*Beneath the Himalayas*

# the BENEath
# himalayas

**JASPER L. McPHAIL**

**CONVENTION PRESS**
Nashville, Tennessee

A publication of the
Foreign Mission Board
Richmond, Virginia

© 1966 • CONVENTION PRESS
Nashville, Tennessee
All rights reserved

522-157

# Preface

In the world today, the Indo-Pakistani subcontinent is the most populous region that is open to the preaching of the gospel of Christ. Less than one half the size of the United States in area, it has approximately six hundred million people, of whom 2.3 percent are Christian.

The giants, India and Pakistan, are not the only important countries in this large area beneath the Himalayas. Geographically, the subcontinent includes India, East and West Pakistan, the two provinces of Kashmir and Jammu (which are claimed by both India and Pakistan), and the countries of Nepal, Sikkim, Bhutan, Ceylon, and the eastern part of Afghanistan.

It was to India that William Carey, the father of modern missions, went. A British Baptist, he lighted the torch which sent its glow around the globe. His influence touched the hearts of Adoniram Judson and Luther Rice, and through them led Baptists of America to organize into supporting mission organizations. In 1836, almost simultaneously, they opened three mission stations in India. Then, the splitting of the Baptists of America into northern and southern conventions in 1845 brought to a close the involvement of Southern Baptist churches in the task of winning India to Christ.

In response to Christ's command, "into all the world," Baptist groups all over the world have poured thousands of lives and dollars into the subcontinent. One out of every four Protestant Christians there today is a Baptist. It has the second largest group of Baptists in the world, only the United States having more. As Baptists in the subcontinent take up the challenge of preaching the gospel throughout their homeland, they look to other Baptist groups for support in personnel, counsel, and prayer.

To Southern Baptists, they seem to say, "Where have you been for the last one hundred and twenty years, Rip Van Winkle?"

This book gives a fleeting glance at the religions, peoples, and culture in the land that lies below the Himalayas. Southern Baptists must face the responsibility of witnessing to that democratic stronghold in one of the most critical times in Asian history. If the book can be used by God to raise the mist that shrouds the area from the vision of Southern Baptists, then its purpose will be accomplished. If it results in the bringing of anyone to Christ or in the bringing of anyone to a deeper commitment to him, that will be earth's sublimest reward.

I would like to thank the Indians and Pakistanis who have inspired many sections of this book. The lessons I have learned from them far exceed any contribution I have made. My appreciation goes to all the correspondents of the various Baptist bodies in India and Pakistan who have supplied much information for the book. Special appreciation goes to Miss Genevieve Greer for seeing the book through from start to finish.

                                                                JASPER L. MCPHAIL

# Contents

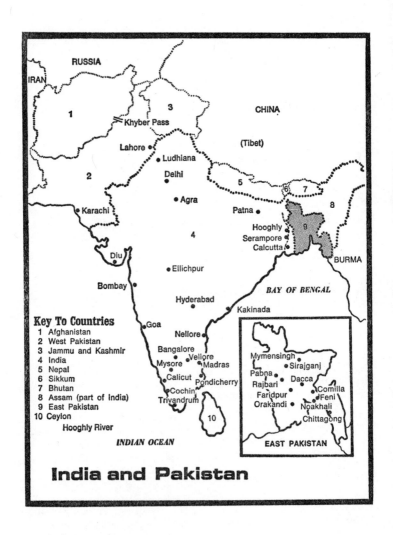

RUSSIA

IRAN

CHINA

1

3

Khyber Pass

(Tibet)

Lahore

Ludhiana

Delhi

5

2

6

7

Agra

8

Karachi

Patna

Hooghly

9

Serampore

Calcutta

Diu

BURMA

Ellichpur

Bombay

BAY OF BENGAL

Hyderabad

Kakinada

**Key To Countries**

Goa

1 Afghanistan
2 West Pakistan
3 Jammu and Kashmir
4 India
5 Nepal
6 Sikkum
7 Bhutan
8 Assam (part of India)
9 East Pakistan
10 Ceylon
 Hooghly River

Nellore

Bangalore

Vellore

Mysore

Madras

Calicut

Pondicherry

Cochin

Trivandrum

Mymensingh

Sirajganj

Pabna

Dacca

Rajbari

Comilla

Faridpur

Feni

Orakandi

Noakhali

Chittagong

10

EAST PAKISTAN

*INDIAN OCEAN*

# India and Pakistan

# 1 Birth of Two Nations

"Is the Ku Klux Klan very active in your area of the U.S.A.?" The question shocked me into an upright position. Members of the Christian Hospital staff in Vellore, India, were resting around a coffee table after a hard day. The inquirer was a brilliant intern, the daughter of an official of the Communist party in India. I realized that she was not joking.

"What makes you ask that?" I teased, smiling.

"Well, my father has some books about the Klan. I read some of them when I was young, and I've just always wondered," she replied. "I've never been able to understand the reason for such an organization."

I explained that although I was from the Deep South, I had never seen a Klansman. She seemed at least to believe that the KKK did not ride every night. Everyone at the table was intent on the conversation.

Just as I relaxed for another long sip of the incomparable South Indian coffee, she leaned across the table again and hesitatingly said, "Do you mind if I ask you something?"

"No," I said. "I have nothing to hide, and I am not here as a defender of everything that exists in America. Go ahead."

"Uh! It's about the race situation in the States." I winced, and her eyes danced as if she knew she had cornered me. "Does a white person ever marry a Negro where you came from?" she continued.

I looked across the table at her penetratingly. The other eight pairs of eyes at the table were focused on us, and the silence was painful.

"Yes, Amma," I slowly began. "Just as often as a Kerala Brahman marries a Tamilian. Just as often as an Indian marries a Pakistani. Just as often as an Arab marries a Jew."

The silence deepened. Then slowly she began to smile until she had a broad grin. "You know, I'd never really thought of it that way. Thank you," she said, as we all smiled and relaxed again.

"Never mind," I said. "The problem is universal. We all have our prejudices. They just are easier to see in other people."

"Are you a typical American?" someone else asked.

"You folks really specialize in hard questions!" I laughed. "I guess we all think that we are average. But you shouldn't think of me as typical. If you do, you will miss the fascination of the variety of Americans. Before I answer your question, please describe for me a typical Indian."

Each person looked at the other, and before long all of us were wearing broad grins. They realized that, just as there is no typical Indian, there is no typical American. Eleven of us were sitting around the table, and that many races and tongues were represented.

Two of India's many tribal groups were there. Sinati (sin-OTT-ey) came from Manipur (MAH-ny-poor) in the troubled Naga (NAH-ga) Hills area. He was short with broad, coarse facial features, an easy smile, and a slight Mongoloid feature in his eyes. Zok (zock) was

tall and slender, unmistakably Indian, with mild traces
of an Oriental ancestry. He was a Lushai (LOO-shy)
from the peaceful hills of Tripura. Both were Christians,
as are many of the area's tribal people, most of whom
are Baptists and Presbyterians. Both had long ago given
up their traditional tribal dress for Western clothes. Their
mother tongues were tribal languages.

Lalitha (la-LEET-tha) was intelligent and unassum-
ing. Her language was Malayalam. Long, black hair,
glistening with coconut oil, was smoothed back from
her forehead and twisted into an elegant roll on the back
of her head. Her plain cotton sari was unusual for a
woman who comes from the very icing of India's Hindu
caste system. It was a symbol of the political affiliation of
her father, who had given up the highest social and
religious position in India, and one of its greatest for-
tunes. From the top rung of the ladder, he had revolted
against the caste system with its privileged few and its
deprived millions. He became an outcaste though he had
once been "one with God." He became a common man
where once he was wealthy. He suffered imprisonment
where he had once known palatial comforts. Explain
it? He was dedicated to a cause—the Communist party.

Most of Lalitha's female cousins were married by the
age of sixteen. They were never allowed outside their
own community. Their parents considered higher education unnecessary for girls. Lalitha was the first woman
from this family, which can trace its lineage back for
thousands of years, to leave the confines of the community, and she was the first to study medicine.

Akbar (OC-bar) was a Muslim of Persian ancestry.
He ate no pork. His language was Urdu (UHR-doo).
Typical of India's color consciousness, his manner seemed

, and aloof because of his fair skin and green eyes. lim society claims to have no class distinction, but was arrogant toward the South Indian Muslims, who were obviously from the Dravidian race which was converted to Islam by the sword during the days of Muslim conquest. He was one of over forty million Muslims who elected to stay in India following partitioning.

Saroj (suh-ROJ) had a lovely countenance, the bright red *telak* (TEE-luk) in her forehead giving her an exotic look. Her coal-black hair was cut in shoulder-length style. Long pendant earrings of gold added needed length to her round face. She was wearing a silk Punjabi style of dress, which is a ballooning type of pajama pants fitting tightly at the ankles and a chemise dress that comes to the knees. A superfluous-appearing piece of matching fabric was draped across the front of her shoulders, much like a stole worn backwards. She was a strict vegetarian and, before coming to medical school, had never eaten in the presence of non-Brahmans. Her tones were soft and modest. Her mother tongue was Marathi (mah-RAH-tee).

Rachel looked as if she could have come from anywhere in the subcontinent or the Middle East. Except for the typical South Indian sari, nothing about her localized her origin. Her shoulder-length hair, uncommon in the deep South, looked more like that of Bombay women. None of the girls at the table wore long, braided pigtails like most South Indian girls. I was surprised to learn that Rachel was a Jewish girl whose forefathers came to Cochin, India, before the time of Christ. Except for her religious affiliation and a slightly arched nose, she was completely Indianized. She had learned both Hebrew and Malayalam and had forgotten which was her mother tongue. Like Akbar, she ate no pork.

Gari (GAR-ry), the six-foot, five-inch giant of the campus, was a Punjabi Sikh who was reared in the city of Delhi. His mother tongue was Hindustani with a mixture of Punjabi. Largely an agricultural people, the Sikhs are sturdy and strong. They have the ruggedness characteristic of those who live in the open. In most of the major cities they seem to have a corner on the taxicab business and are daredevil drivers. They are recognized by their multicolored turbans and their woven beards. In religion, they are strongly monotheistic Hindus. Gari had cut off his long hair and beard and had given up wearing the turban. He represents a generation of professional, highly educated Sikhs who are loosening the externals of their religion.

Kurien (koo-re-un) was a Syrian Christian from Kerala. His ancestors came from Syria to the western coast of India during the first century after Christ. Down through the ages they maintained family purity by prohibiting intermarriage with other Indians. Even today their church services are in the Syrian language, although, long ago, they adopted Malayalam as their mother tongue. Kurien's people are the financiers and merchants of Kerala state. As Indian society goes, they are considered to be the highest ranking non-Hindus in the nation. They have always been known for an emphasis on higher education, and many of them hold important posts throughout the Indian Union. They, along with the Parsees, tend to be the most westernized people in the subcontinent. Because of their intellect and business sense, they have often been called the Jews of India.

John was, in many ways, a more typical Indian than

any of the others. His mother tongue was Telugu. Like
almost 85 per cent of India's people, he came from a
village in a rural area. His family was in the outcaste
group, which makes up one fifth of the nation's population. At one time they were not allowed to live within
the village walls or to travel on the main roads. Always
crouching and sneaking along the back ways for fear
of defiling caste Hindus, they could not even let their
shadow fall on them. In many respects, they were treated
as victims of leprosy were in New Testament times.
There was never a kind word for them. They were
cursed and abused.

Even though caste has been outlawed in India, it is
still as much in vogue in the villages as segregation is
in some sections of the United States. John's father had
no hope of rising above this status. Even though he had
a deep hunger for worship, he was not allowed to worship in the Hindu temple. By Hindu rules, he was
denied access to society and to God. He could have no
ambition for his son. Generation after generation, the
outcastes were expected to grind out their karma
(CUR-mah, the sum total of one's actions, which Hindus
believe determines their station in life in the next incarnation). Their station in life was the world's most miser-
able; their only escape, death.

One day John's father came home from his leather
work with a spring in his step. The sad, dull countenance
was gone. He beamed as he told his family of a new life
that was possible in Christ. Even outcastes could find
acceptance and forgiveness. They had equal status with
others before God. They could even enter his temples
and worship. No longer would they have to eat the
crumbs of idolatry and beat drums all night to gods of

stone to whom they were not allowed to bow down. This outcaste family, as many others among them, found new life in Christ because a Baptist pastor gave up a comfortable pulpit in America and brought the long-delayed message.

The young son, at the time of his baptism, changed his name to John. Sent to a mission school for a Christian education, he grew and matured there. He proved that people of an outcaste background are not laggards intellectually. His excellent record and sterling character won him a seat in medical school. He plans to work in a mission hospital among his own people. He is their symbol of hope. They need him for more than just his medicine.

Around just one coffee table I glimpsed the complex society that composes Pakistan and India.

Here and there throughout the subcontinent are tucked away little communities of different language and racial groups. There is a fairly good-sized Parsee (Zoroastrians who have migrated to India from Persia) community in northern India and West Pakistan. Small Oriental communities are found in the cities of Calcutta, Delhi, and Bombay. There is even a quaint Armenian community in Calcutta. Near Hyderabad (HY-der-ah-BAD), India, is a settlement of Africans whose fathers were brought there centuries ago as slaves for the Muslim rulers. All of these communities, isolated from their motherlands and religions, challenge Southern Baptists to tell them of Christ.

Age-old tensions and rivalries still affect daily life in the subcontinent in a thousand ways. These often are the driving forces behind occurrences the missionary is at a loss to explain. Muslim Pakistan with its ten million

Hindus and Hindu India with its 45 million Muslims
are, almost twenty years after the partitioning of the
subcontinent of India into the two countries of India
and Pakistan, still feeling the "fallout" of intense hate
that erupted during that period. But during the crisis of
the partitioning and even today Christians are witnessing
the power of reconciliation which we have in Christ.
In the past, India's Nehru paid a glowing tribute to the
Christians of India and Pakistan because they ministered
impartially during those dark days. Coming from all
backgrounds of race, religion, and caste, the Christians,
as they labored side by side, showed how they had
been miraculously welded together in the bonds of love
as Christian brothers. They forgot the things of the past
and gave themselves to the task that was before them,
a task that continues to challenge them.

From the time I had read Rudyard Kipling, the
mystery of the great subcontinent called India had
seemed unfathomable to me. Study into its culture and
religion still left me with a sense of mystery.

The people are talkative. They are famous for their
ability to narrate. The village narrator can hold his
audience enthralled for endless hours. I fold my legs
and listen as they reveal their mysterious land to me. I
would like to share with you some of what I have heard
from their own lips.

*An Indian Viewpoint*

"In less than a year over one million people were
murdered in cold blood!"

The voice, which sounded like that of a European
woman, came from Room 205 of the hospital as I
approached. I lingered at the door, hoping to hear more.

An Indian nurse walked briskly out of the room, her crisp white sari crackling as she whisked past me.

"May I go in?" I asked.

"Surely," the nurse replied, and quipped over her shoulder, "She is in a talking mood today."

I hardly expected to find a petite little Indian woman stroking her long, graying hair. I introduced myself, explaining that I was one of the surgeons assigned to her case.

"I am a doctor, too," she proudly announced, "and at the moment I am feeling too well to have you poking around my gallbladder! Sit down."

She was easy to talk to. Her twinkling eyes radiated a "soul peace" that was almost angelic. The mellow lines of her bronze face reflected a character tempered in the crucible of life to withstand the relentless crises of famine and flood and war. She spoke in soft and gracious tones about current world affairs, the Christian work in the nation, and the need for doctors and nurses in rural India.

Several attempts to get her back to her words at the time of my entrance failed. Then suddenly she exclaimed, "Oh, you want me to tell you about my experiences during the partitioning of India and Pakistan!" She continued:

"It is embarrassing to tell these things to foreigners. You think of us as being nonviolent, like Gandhiji. You people in the West never really knew what took place during the partitioning. The international press tells us in India when a child is treated unjustly in the United States, but I'm sure you never knew how many people were killed here in 1947. The official estimate was a million—more people than the United States lost in both

world wars. The actual number of murders was probably
two or three times that.

"At the time, I was working right on the border of
India and West Pakistan. I saw the streets literally run
with blood as mobs clashed and fought until not a man
was left standing. I saw babies snatched from their
mothers and torn to bits. I saw whole families and even
whole villages destroyed. Nearly seven million people
were left homeless and hungry. In the crowded, unclean
camps of the refugees, rampant epidemics took their
toll. The misery and suffering were beyond imagination."
She spoke as only an eyewitness can, her eyes kindling
at the memory.

"And what were you doing during all this?" I ventured.

She managed a faint smile. "Well, the most they could
do to a little old spinster doctor was murder her, so I
decided to stay. The wounded needed care. As long as
strength and bandages lasted, I cared for wounded people on both sides of the fighting. When I was too tired
to move, I would lie down and pray that God would
have mercy on us all. It was a marvelous opportunity
for us few Christians in India to witness, in the middle
of this conflict, to the love of Christ."

"This is a chilling story," I said, "especially when it
comes from one who was in the thick of it. But beyond
the mere facts, tell me the cause of it all."

"To do that, I would have to go back for centuries,"
she mused.

Of course, I knew that the fighting was between the
Hindus and Muslims, but still none of it made sense to
me. The subcontinent looks so peaceful now that it is hard
to believe that it was torn by civil war less than twenty
years ago.

The little doctor had spoken of India's George Washington, Gandhiji (giving Gandhi's name the customary ending that denotes honor). This guiding light for over a quarter of a century was snuffed out by a Hindu fanatic who thought he was doing his country a favor, she told me. Three shots pierced the silence of the dusk, and Gandhiji lay crumpled in the dust before a stunned and shocked world.

Looking much like a New Testament character, Gandhi was an enigma to most people. He lived primarily on raw fruits and vegetables and goat's milk, seldom eating anything cooked. He never ate meat. His clothing was the plainest of homespun fabrics, and he usually wore sandals on bare feet. Giving up his family fortune because he considered poverty a virtue, he reserved Mondays for fasting, silence, and prayer. In a modern age of industrialization, science, and technology, he bewildered contemporary world leaders by advocating a return to cottage industries and the land. To him freedom meant freedom from hunger and unemployment, as well as from a colonial power.

Throughout the land Gandhi became a symbol of independence. He was revered by millions, and unfortunately worshiped by many. They bestowed on him the title of "Mahatma," meaning "the great-souled one." To Hindus it signifies one who is impartial to all mankind without regard for race, creed, color, or sex.

In an era when most world powers indulged in two great wars in order to maintain the status quo, the little man called Gandhiji accomplished independence for his country without raising a sword. The British had, in their 200-year reign over India, become accustomed to putting down armed rebellion by force. They were less adept at psychological warfare. Gandhiji's methods were passive resistance and civil disobedience. His long fasts drew the attention of all of India to his cause. When the British jailed or punished him, he only emerged stronger and more determined.

Gandhi was a product of his civilization in the broadest sense. His victories could have been won only in India, and only he could have won them. Dedicated to the task before him, he was a sensitive student of Indian history and psychology. One can understand him only in the context of Indian culture.

He was not the first to win an entire nation by psychological maneuvers. There were his forefathers, the Aryans, who entered India through Khyber Pass about 2500 B.C. They found there a well-developed urban civilization. Excavations at Mohenjo-Daro and Harappa (moh-HEN-jo-DAH-roh and ha-RAP-ah) in Pakistan show that those Dravidian cities had one of the earliest highly organized urban societies known to archaeologists.

The Aryans, on the other hand, were a pastoral people known for simple living and high thinking. At the height of their culture, about 2000 B.C., they produced the *Rigveda*, one of the earliest books known to humanity. The sacred book of the Hindus, it shows that the Aryans probably brought the Hindu religion with them into India from the highlands of Central Asia. As they entered the northern part of the subcontinent, they were outnumbered by the highly organized Dravidians. Therefore, their chief weapon was their intellect. The fair Aryans segregated themselves from the dark-skinned Dravidians and began to weave about themselves a religious philosophy that would put them on top of the social heap.

Previously, there had been no caste system. Gradually,

the Aryans divided society according to special needs.
The Brahman class, ministering to the religious needs of
the people, developed a complicated system of sacrifices
and verbal rituals. The rest of the society viewed its
members with such awe and reverence that Brahmans
came to be considered "one with God." Other castes
arose and took their places on the ladder of society.
Political rulers and kings made up the second highest
caste as the need arose for administrators over conquered territories. The third caste was composed of people engaged in trade, commerce, agriculture, and hus-
bandry. The fourth caste was the servant class. Through
the centuries hundreds of subcastes gradually developed
from these four caste groups. About one fifth of the
population, left outside the realm of caste, became known
as "outcastes" or "untouchables." Today they are called
"scheduled castes" or, as Gandhi liked to call them,
"children of God" (Harijans, HA-re-johns).

Over a period of fifteen years the Aryans elevated
themselves to the cream of the social system. Though
they seldom resorted to battle, they extended their influence over the vast subcontinent, from Persia to China
and from the Himalaya Mountains to the sea.

In his own nation's history Gandhi learned his first
lesson in warless victory. It was to India's history also
that he looked for lessons from a ruler named Asoka
(a-SO-kah). Hardly any other ruler in all of the world's
history can be compared to Asoka. H. G. Wells, the historian, considers him to be the world's greatest king.
Wherein lay his greatness?

Silencing the war drum, he introduced the novel
scheme of governing his subjects by the rod of righteous-
ness instead of by the sword. The greatness of a ruler

depends not on the vastness of his empire, he wrote, but on the mental and physical progress of his people. He provided wells for the villagers, hospitals for the sick, and highways for the travelers. At a time of intense religious upheaval two hundred and fifty years before Christ, he declared a secular state with religious tolerance to all. Religious tolerance in a secular state was his most priceless legacy to India. Asoka ruled out war as a solution to international problems. The first to appoint a "peace corps" to West Asian countries and Ceylon, he ushered in an era of nonviolence and conquest through love. His messages are engraved on rocks and pillars throughout India.

In Room 205, I glanced at my watch. Two hours had passed. I had been spellbound by my master storyteller's fascinating account of enchanting India, but I still had not solved her problem of jaundice.

Grudgingly, I arose. Looking forward to another visit, I remarked: "That is an intriguing story, but so far you haven't explained why all of the barbarities of the partitioning."

"Oh," she grinned, "then we're even! I do not understand all the barbarities of surgeons, either. We both can do some more explaining!"

At a later visit I learned from her that a revival of Hinduism followed Asoka's Buddhist rule in India. A strong Hindu government was formed. Again, the psychological warfare of the Brahmans won the victory. During this period the Hindu Puranas (myths and legends) were written. The clever Brahmans incorporated into them a legend stating that the kings were sent by the gods to rid India of the Buddhists. By a slow cold war, and occasionally through fierce battle, the soldier and ruler castes reclaimed all of India for the Brahmans, while the Brahmans themselves sat by hypocritically involved in "the deeper things of the spirit."

My patient and I pondered together the deep cleavage which religious differences have caused between peoples down through the centuries. Whereas one would expect religious men to be instruments of God's peace, they have many times instigated history's bloodiest wars and committed the most heinous crimes.

"How do you explain it?" I coaxed.

She told me of a Muslim conqueror who marched into the northern part of the Indian subcontinent less than a century after the prophet Mohammed lived. This war was followed in the tenth century by other Muslim invasions. The chief conqueror among them not only plundered India's wealth and subdued her politically, but destroyed many Hindu temples, robbing them of precious gold, silver, and gems. He crushed so many idols that he became known as "the image breaker." The stage was set for deep-seated Hindu-Muslim hostility.

Two centuries later another Muslim conqueror tried to capture the whole of the subcontinent. He forced his religion, at spear point, down the throats of many frightened Hindus. Many others changed their religion in order to escape heavy taxes levied on non-Muslims, or in order to gain employment as clerks and attendants to the Muslims. By the end of A.D. 1300, Hindu power was banished from the north, leaving only a remnant in southern India.

In the sixteenth century, a Muslim emperor called Akbar the Great brought a new day in Hindu-Muslim relationships. He was merciful and gracious toward the conquered. To his family he was affectionate, humane, and compassionate. Like the prophet Mohammed, he seems to have been tolerant in the selection of his wives, for he is reputed to have chosen a Muslim, a Christian, a Hindu, and a Parsee. Akbar founded a new sect that, unlike most of Islam, featured universal toleration. He also abolished the heavy tax on Hindus and allowed them freedom of worship.

The subcontinent gained much from its Muslim invaders. Shah Jahan (ja-HAAN) built the world's most solemn building of grandeur, the Taj Mahal in Agra (tahj mah-HALL in AH-gra), northern India. Its gorgeous lines of pure white marble are decorated with mosaics of many-colored precious stones. He also built in Delhi the famous Peacock Throne, which is worth more than fifteen million dollars, and in Lahore (lah-HOAR) the beautiful Shalimar Gardens. Throughout the subcontinent are gorgeous buildings, a legacy of the superb Muslim architecture of this period.

Oppression by Akbar's successor led to renewed feuds and deeper cleavage between the Hindus and Muslims. This fierce anti-Muslim feeling, coupled with decay within Islamic rule, set the stage for the entrance of a third power. Fear of revival of Muslim rule caused the Hindu rulers to negotiate alliances with the British, who were interested in gaining a foothold in India. The entrance of the British brought an end to Muslim domination.

"This was an interesting turn of events," I remarked, as my storyteller spoke of the beginning of British rule in the subcontinent.

"Yes," the woman mused, "something like sleeping with the fox in order to keep from going to bed with the lion! Nevertheless, it gave the Hindus a letup from Muslim cruelties. Yet, it opened the way for more subtle psychological indignities."

She laughed. "Of course, you know that America was only discovered because Europe wanted a route to India! Then only six years after its discovery, Vasco da Gama discovered the sea route to India around the Cape of Good Hope. Afterward, the subcontinent became dotted with European ports, each of them a little island of European culture. The Portuguese were in the small city-districts of Calicut, Goa, Hooghly, Diu, and Chittagong. The Danes had a small enclave in Serampore. The Dutch had small areas in the state of Bengal. The British were in large areas of the state of Bengal and Madras, and the French had the city-district of Pondicherry (pon-dee-shay-REE). All of these were established within about a hundred years.

"The foreign powers were in command. We Indians were just spectators, or paid fighters in their wars. We watched battles, massacres, deceptions, and treaties, followed by further corruption, unjust plunder, and the extraction of heavy tribute. Why, they even exacted heavy duty from Indians in the east in order to finance their wars against Indians who were holding out in the south. I hope you won't misunderstand, but these and other injustices started the prejudice most Easteners feel toward the West today. Maybe that's the reason we never give anyone our complete trust. The coming of the first missionaries coincided with all of this, and in many Indian minds they came in the same parcel."

"But, you know, just as a spectator I can see many benefits of British rule," I commented halfheartedly.

"Oh, yes. No one would deny that," she agreed. "Even

though they made us feel inferior, they also benefited us. I've already said that they freed us from a decadent Muslim rule. They gave us one of the best railroad systems in Asia, a good postal system, an organized educational system, an international language, protection from neighboring invaders. But a wounded inner conscience is long in healing. We shall not easily forget the acts of bigotry stemming from the assumption that the white race is superior." She stared into space, looking pained.

"That gives me insight into many things I have observed here, but so far I am not completely enlightened on the Hindu-Muslim conflict," I said, trying to guide her away from Indo-British wounds.

"To get a true picture of the Muslim side of the story, you should meet Abdul Fazal, a Pakistani friend of mine," she suggested. "He understands his people better than I do, and he's coming next week to bring his little girl for heart surgery."

"That's a good bargain," I jested. "You introduce me to him, and you can rest. Besides, tomorrow we are going to remove the stone from your bile duct. You won't feel like talking much for a few days."

## A Pakistani Viewpoint

The following week Abdul Fazal arrived in Vellore with his wife and little girl and what looked like a whole boxcar full of luggage. They had come prepared for a three-month stay, with clothes, cooking utensils, and even food. They planned to take an apartment in the town while little Farah had open-heart surgery for correction of a birth defect. The waiting list for such operations was so long that often several months of waiting were required.

"You are an unusual father. To be so devoted to your daughter is not common in this land," I remarked to Abdul Fazal.

The tall, almond-skinned Pakistani dropped his eyes toward his lap. His brow furrowed. As he raised his eyes after a long silence, I inquired, "Do you have other children?"

"We did have," he said in a melancholy tone. "We had two sons. Both were killed during the days of the partitioning. Oh, what foolishness that was!" A sad, faraway look came to his moistened eyes, which were emerald green, an unusual color among Pakistanis.

"I know how much any Muslim treasures his sons, Mr. Fazal. It must have been a tremendous shock to you."

"Yes, but it has deepened my sense of values and appreciation. Little Farah was born after we moved to Pakistan. It seemed as if merciful Allah was trying to compensate for our grief. Shortly after her birth we noticed that she had blue lips and fingernails. The doctor told us she had congenital heart disease."

"That would have embittered many people," I remarked.

He shook his head. "Why should it? It was Allah's will. It is my duty to accept it. However, it has caused us to be overindulgent toward our child."

Abdul Fazal stood up to leave, his classic Persian features betraying his ancestry. The little girl clutched his pants leg with her blue fingers. As they walked down the hall she was obviously short of breath, and Fazal picked her up and carried her.

I felt as if I had known Fazal a long time, but he was always businesslike and reserved. I wanted to hear his account of the partitioning, but feared he would think I was intruding if I appeared too premature or brash about it.

Two days later he suddenly appeared in my office door, politely removed his fez, and asked courteously, "May I come in?"

"Surely. You're just the man I want to see," I assured him, and whispered an order to the office boy, hoping that coffee would relax my visitor for my gentle prodding.

"Please, do you have time to tell me of the partitioning?" I coaxed. "I am afraid that I do not understand it."

He gave a wry grin and said: "Neither do we. You know, it's something like a man and wife who have bickered for forty years. Then one day they get a divorce, but neither one of them can recall how it all started." We laughed together, and he continued, "Then after the divorce, they settle down next door to each other, and the bickering continues. The only difference is that now it is across the fence." We chuckled together again.

Back as early as World War I, members of the Muslim League in India were keenly aware of their minority status, he told me. To preserve their rights and have political power, they had to be organized and united.

Under British rule, Muslim domination ceased; and the Muslim is not likely to be content in a role of subjection. Whereas the Hindu changed his ways and adapted to a Western overlord, Muslims hugged the memory of their glorious past. They were further humiliated because the Hindus threw off their Muslim-Hindu culture and returned to the more ancient era of Hinduism. This trend was noticed in music, art, architecture, and language.

These changes were ultimately responsible for the political cleavage which resulted in the emergence of Pakistan. The Hindus built for themselves a new and distinct culture and were planning a new India along Hindu lines. The Muslims, an island of cultural isolation, were politically and economically powerless, even though they formed one fourth of the entire population of the subcontinent. They had no place for themselves. Many Hindu thinkers saw no reason why Muslims should not be absorbed into Hindu India just as many other minority groups had been.

The majority of Indian Muslims were in no mood to accept absorption. They wanted to live in India as Muslims, with no divided allegiance toward Allah. They purified their Islamic theology and began to shun all forms of Hindu culture. Muslims and Hindus began to dress more distinctly different, and Muslims began to think of themselves as a nation within a nation.

As a safeguard against Hindu domination, the Muslims demanded proper representation in government. Soon they developed the conviction that only political independence could guarantee them a distinct existence. They feared that after the British left they would be hopelessly engulfed in a predominantly Hindu India. Under the capable leadership of Mohammed Ali Jinnah, they were organized effectively and were able to progress steadily in achieving their goal. In 1947, it was decided to set up two separate nations, the Dominion of Pakistan and the Dominion of India.

"It was truly a day of triumph for us. We had suffered all the indignities of a minority group and of deposed rulers. Allah delivered us," Mr. Fazal said with deep pride, his eyes glowing.

"But all was not well in the days that followed." His contenance darkened. "The brutality, plunder, rape, murder, and arson would have shocked even the Crusaders."

"This is an interesting revelation to me," I remarked, "for your writers say very little of it in their works. What about the famous Eastern tolerance and spirituality?"

"Oh, you have been reading our history and philosophy books!" he exclaimed. With a look that let me know I was on forbidden ground, he added, "You are much more likely to find tolerance and spirituality in our books than on our streets." I dared say no more.

As we walked out to the veranda from the office the last few orange-colored rays of the day spotlighted an old Muslim fort on a nearby hill. I saw it as a symbol of a historic past, the seal of an era.

## Order Out of Chaos

It was a bad day to travel. There were streamers across the roads everywhere. From every building, tree, and post, bright-colored paper flapped in the breeze. Loudspeakers blasted haunting music at too frequent intervals. Everyone seemed to be in the streets, adding his bit to the merriment and confusion. Cars were barely able to creep through the masses of people. An ageless and weary society was rejuvenated by the thought of freedom. It was August 15, Independence Day.

In 1947, the subcontinent had emerged from its bloodbath in quest of freedom. Even the humblest village peasant was emotionally involved in the struggle. The holiday gave everyone good reason for a festival celebration. For us who watched, it called to memory the birth of two nations—two great Asian democracies—within our own lifetime. We, too, were mysteriously charmed into the spell of the day and were trying feebly to sing the national anthem.

Pakistan became a new and powerful nation without even the physical facilities for beginning a new government. She had to build a government where there was none. There were not even tables and chairs and stationery for the officials. Many of the most important merchants and industrialists left the country, and refugees by the millions poured in. It is a tribute to the genius of a noble people that order was soon brought out of chaos.

Today Pakistan is vibrant with life and vigor. She has a democratic government that is fashioned along the spiritual and ethical lines of Islam but denies accusations that she is becoming a theocratic state. Non-Muslim ministers and legislators are included among her officials. Progress is seen on all sides.

The Pakistanis, with their tradition of bureaucracy and Roman law, established a smooth-running government and wrote their own constitution. Their nation is a federation of provinces, and there is little federal intervention in provincial affairs. Pakistan is an independent member of the British Commonwealth, and as such claims Queen Elizabeth to be independently queen of Pakistan and queen of the United Kingdom.

The making of the united nation of Pakistan can be traced to the high price she paid for freedom. It took several decades of united struggle for the people to free themselves from the British and the Hindus. Every Pakistani had to participate in the struggle, and often made great sacrifices. Scarcely is there a family among

Pakistan's seven million refugees that has not lost a son, a daughter, or an aged father or mother, or some other relative in the partitioning. People are there who are sole survivors of large families. Many others never reached the border of their "Promised Land." A nation that has suffered so much cannot but feel a sense of unity and achievement.

Had Christians been willing to pay the same price to establish the kingdom of Christ in non-Christian lands I believe victory would be ours!

India, with much more equipment and many more trained government officials than Pakistan, set about at the same time putting her democratic socialism into effect. Her constitution provides for a secular state with freedom of religion for all. Equal rights are claimed for all, regardless of caste, creed, race, religion, or sex. This provision has given new hope even to the Hindus who were accustomed to being bound by rules of caste. Now, potentially, anyone can attain the highest rung on the ladder.

India is a republic and an independent member of the British Commonwealth. Justly proud of her achievements, she is conscious of her importance as a world power.

Together, Pakistan and India represent the greatest mass of free people in the world. They are a democratic bulwark against communism in Asia. To them much of non-Communist Asia looks for guidance and leadership. The other countries of the subcontinent nestle snugly on the borders of the two nations. Pakistan and India are their only security against the Red Aggressor.

Tibet within the last decade has been engulfed behind the Bamboo Curtain. The tiger is still at the door of the subcontinent on its northeastern borders. Encased within the Himalayas, the Buddhist kingdom of Nepal, Sikkim, and Bhutan keenly feel the pressure of China's closeness. Their hope lies in the strength of India and Pakistan to stand against communism.

Jammu and Kashmir, with a predominence of Muslims but with a sizable Hindu citizenry and a good many Buddhists, sit as the great thorn in the flesh for India-Pakistan negotiations for peace. Both sides want the area and are so emotional over the issue that the deadlock of wills seems impossible to break.

Tropical Ceylon, the Hawaii of Asia, is just a few miles off the southern tip of the subcontinent. Even though her government is Buddhist and the avowed state religion is Buddhism, she has a sizable population of Hindus of Indian ancestry. Ceylon plays an important role in helping to form plans for an unaligned Asian solidarity. The island nation has also produced one of Asia's greatest Christian thinkers, D. T. Niles. In a country that discourages any Christian witness, and is closed to most mission work, it is to men such as he that the mantle of leadership has fallen.

Because most of the countries that fringe the subcontinent are closed to missionary witness to the gospel of Christ, approaches other than traditional ways of mission work are necessary. Dedicated diplomats, educators, scientists, technologists, and medical personnel who do not travel under the name of missionary could penetrate their walls. There is need for concentrated effort in India and Pakistan before the doors swing shut. A strong witness in those two major countries would undoubtedly, because of present-day travel and communication, send tidal waves of influence to the fringes.

## 2 The Quest
## for Men's Minds

"Something within me kept telling me that what I was doing was terribly wrong."

The voice was that of Mr. Srivastava (sre-VAS-ta-va). He was weary from a fifteen-hundred-mile pilgrimage for "soul peace." He could not sit still in his chair. His reddened eyes glared like those of someone on the verge of mental breakdown. He had not slept for days. His palms were sweaty. Agitated, apprehensive, filled with a guilt anxiety, he was as taut as a banjo string. One more turn of the wheel of life, and he would snap.

I asked him to tell me what had brought him so far, past many other hospitals, to ours. Gradually, over a period of three days, he poured out a heartrending story of sin and its harvest, a harvest that was wrecking him physically, mentally, and spiritually.

Twisting a handkerchief until the threads whined, he began telling me his physical symptoms. It was apparent to me that they were the outward signs of a psychological conflict, probably a conflict with a spiritual basis. I let him unravel his story without too much interference or offensive probing.

The man had gone to the Hindu priest of his village over a year before and poured out his story of despair. The priest had remarked, "What you have done is not a sin. You are only normal. A mistake has merely overtaken you. What you should do is to forget about it."

According to the unwritten code in that particular community the priest was right. Even though prostitution had been outlawed in Indian temple worship, not all obeyed the law. The temple girls practiced their profession with little emotional involvement. It had been an accepted part of life in Srivastava's village for centuries, and no one seemed to get a guilt complex. Why was Srivastava any different?

He tried to justify himself by saying that all of his friends were doing the same. He tried to bury himself in devotion and prayers to the temple gods. He tried to level his balance by performing good deeds. But his spiritual turmoil only deepened. He was in a room with no exit provided by his traditional beliefs.

I said very little during the three days he told his story. He told how he had sought tranquility by studying the teachings of Buddha. Sin was supposed to be only ignorance. Then, salvation must be the result of knowledge to be found within oneself. In Buddhism as in Hinduism, salvation is said to be by paths of knowledge, work, or devotion. Srivastava had already tried to drink from these dry cisterns. Self-realization brought no release. Every time he looked within himself, his guilt only deepened. He did not find God within.

At the breaking point, he had swallowed his pride and gone to the despised Muslims. There were some very brilliant Muslim doctors nearby, and they treated him with all kinds of tranquilizers and stimulants. But these did not lift his depression. They tried to introduce him to Allah.

Allah's teachings in the Koran minimized his sin, but could not erase his guilt. Unlike most Hindus and Mus-

lims, Srivastava felt a personal responsibility for the
wrong he had done. He could not explain it away by
saying, "Mistakes have overtaken me," or "Allah knows
I am weak and will understand." Allah seemed far away,
harsh, and cold. Fellowship with him would be considered by Muslims a scandal. The doctors spoke of him
as merciful, but Srivastava could find no means of forgiveness. Allah accepted his weakness and asked no more
of him, but provided no escape, no hope.

Srivastava felt estranged from God, and the Koran
did not speak of reconciliation or redemption. It only
required him to confess Allah, make a pilgrimage to
Mecca, the holy city, and join in the battle against all
who did not believe in Allah. By this he could achieve
good standing as a Muslim convert. This Islamic way
was but another road of works—a verbal confession,
obedience to a code, service to an impersonal god. It
was concerned only with external things. There was
nothing in it to change a man's heart and give him a
new one, nothing to rid him of his sinful past and join
him in a forgiving fellowship with a loving, truly merciful
God.

Srivastava was at the end of his rope. Despair closed
in about him. Just as a matter of habit, he had gone
through the Hindu rituals of daily baths, weekly oil
baths, baths in the Ganges River, hoping by sheer
repetition to develop enough faith and hope to break
his spell of despair.

One day a new thought had struck him. What is
Christianity? Is there hope in that religion?

Srivastava was reared in what is known as a Hindu
"joint family." His family consists of his aged grand-
father, all of his uncles and their families, his own father,

his three older brothers with their wives and children, and Srivastava with his bride of eight months. The "joint family" makes no decisions except as a group. It is recognized by law. All income goes into a common pool. Access to property is only in terms of the whole group.

Separation from the group may occur by mutual agreement, but if separation is due to change of religion or breaking with caste codes, the guilty member usually is totally cut off. Actually, there are many advantages to the joint family. It is insurance against old age, sickness, unemployment, or incompetence. Its disadvantage is that it limits individual liberty. All interests must be subordinated to the wishes of the group. Often it stifles ambition and initiative.

Srivastava dreaded the possibility of finding an answer outside his own culture. But, he had thought, why not seek? Life as it was for him was meaningless.

He had never seen a Christian until ten years earlier when he went to the government college in the next town. Three Christian students attended the college, but he knew nothing of their religion. The crowd, Srivastava among them, teased the three just because they were different. He made noises to disturb their Bible study and prayers. He shouted vile remarks at them on the campus. He accused them of allegiance to a foreign government and called them traitors to India. But he did not even know their names.

One morning he had left his home for the first time in weeks. Telling no one, not even his wife, where he was going, he caught a bus for a larger town fifty miles away. He wanted to buy a Bible written in Hindi, his mother tongue.

In the tiny bookshop to which he went, he found no Bible. They were sold out.

"Where can I find one?" he inquired.

"No one else in this area sells them," the shopkeeper replied. "But wait just a minute, I have a few copies of the New Testament."

"What's that?" Srivastava asked, looking puzzled. He barely knew the name Bible and did not know it had two Testaments. After the shopkeeper explained that the New Testament was the part that told of Christ, Srivastava bought a copy. Hiding it beneath his shirt, he caught the bus back to his village.

I have often thought how lucky it was that he could *not* find a Bible. What if he had gotten permanently bogged down in Leviticus? But then, what if there had been no New Testament that day?

Srivastava had pored over the pages. When his father came to his room, he hastily hid the small volume beneath a mat. Like any good Hindu wife, his bride asked no questions. He almost memorized the Sermon on the Mount. Here was a passage that penetrated the shell of religion to its core. The Man who spoke the words of the great Sermon understood the very heart of man. If wrong action is first conceived in the heart or mind, then the thought is behind the deed. If the thought is behind the deed, then the cure must strike at the heart and mind. If the cure must be focused on the inner man, then it cannot be achieved by merely changing the deeds or works. If we cannot save ourselves by works, then only a merciful God can lift us out of our situation.

As he went on and on with his story, I marveled at Srivastava's logic. I marveled at how God's Spirit had

been able to work in the heart of a man through his
Word alone, in the complete absence of a human guide.
I marveled that the Hindu man had been able to cross
the psychological barriers of his culture as well as the
barriers of man's wilful disobedience. Afresh and anew,
I realized that this is truly Christ's ministry. We are
merely his instruments. I could not have brought Srivastava to this stage of his journey. "Not by might, nor
by power, but by my spirit, saith the Lord" (Zech. 4:6)—
nor by persuasion, nor by intellect, nor by mere wishing.

"How did you know that the New Testament con-
tained truth?" I asked.

"I wasn't really convinced at first," he said. "It was
just another possibility of escape from my situation.
But the day I read the first chapter of Romans, I knew."

"Why was that so convincing?"

"I had searched the Gita (GEE-tah), the sacred
scripture of the Hindus, and found much that was true.
But I never found an explanation for my conscience-felt
guilt nor any offer of forgiveness. The Koran of Islam
did not even seem to be aware of my deeper needs.
The Buddha, while reacting to much that was wrong in
Hinduism, has not greatly altered the final answers, and
he has paved the way for an egotistical form of atheism
that leaves man the captain of his own destiny.

"When I read the first chapter of John in the Bible,
it spoke of 'the true Light, which lighteth every man'
(v. 9). Romans 1:19 revealed that I was without excuse.
This explained my guilt. God was speaking directly to
my heart all along. That 'something' which kept telling
me that what I was doing was wrong was that Light. I
believe the New Testament because it coincides with my
experience.

"Even after condemnation there is always a word of hope—'the wages of sin . . . but the gift of God.'"

Two days later Srivastava startled me profoundly when he said in a tantalizing tone, "All roads lead to God." I had thought he was near Christian commitment. I quieted my impatience and settled down to another few days of dialogue.

"How do you know that?" I asked.

"It is what all the holy men in India say," he argued.

"But how do you personally know?" I persisted.

"Well, it seems to me that we are all trying to achieve the same goal. Each road goes a different direction, but they all wind up at the top of the hill."

"Do they?" I said in a low, penetrating tone.

He squirmed in his chair, but no answer came. In his Hindu mind, he had pictured life as a steep and rugged mountain with God sitting on top. Man's quest for God took many forms, but all were trying to reach the top of the same hill. Therefore, he assumed that all religions were the same. In India one hears this statement repeatedly. It is always used when anyone runs out of reasons and falls back on old clichés.

"You are familiar with the Himalayas, aren't you?" I asked.

"Yes, they are near my home. Why?" he said, puzzled.

"Let's suppose that we are standing at the foot of one of those mountains and that God is waiting on top." I cringed at this conception of God, but I was struggling to find familiar ground. "There are many roads that start out from the foot of the mountain, aren't there?"

"Yes."

"Can you see them all the way to the top, or do they disappear as they wind through the undergrowth?"

"They disappear," he said slowly, giving me a suspicious look.

"Don't be uneasy. I am not trying to trap you. I just want you to think. If the roads disappear, how do you know they reach the top?"

"I don't, but I could try one of them and see."

"Yes, and if you reached the end of the road and it did not reach the top, what then?"

"I guess I could turn around and come back and start all over."

"Could you? What if time had run out? What if you had become blinded by that particular way and had lost sight of your quest? What if you were too weary? What if the next road was also a blind alley?"

He gave me a pensive look.

"Why do all these roads get lost in the underbrush?" I asked.

"I guess it is because they must take a winding route up the steep mountain."

"But even then they should reach the top, shouldn't they?" His look did not change, so I continued. "They are man's attempts to reach God. These roads look broad and attractive at the foot of the hill, but up the way they prove insufficient. Man's struggles to build a bridge to God have all ended in frustration. What next?"

"Couldn't all religions get together and figure it out better?" he asked halfheartedly.

"If we had to wait until all men agree on the correct way, none of us would ever find deliverance," I said, smiling. "Then if we at the foot of the hill cannot scale the heights, what alternative is there? Are we to be left struggling in the dust? Do we have to await another incarnation to better our lot in life? How long must we struggle to achieve eternal bliss—nirvana? Or, has a merciful and loving God provided the way?

"Let us go back to our original illustration. God is still on the mountaintop. We are all scattered along the roads at the foot. Not one of us has reached him by our own efforts. Since he is the creator, both the mountain and we are his. He gives us the freedom to go our own ways. But one day he sees our misery and plight. He reaches down in love and mercy and makes a way unto himself. Jesus Christ is that Way."

He looked convinced, but then remarked: "If God could provide a way in Christ, surely he could provide a way for all those other roads to reach the top. Isn't he that powerful?"

"Surely, he is. But you're trying to force God to answer your problem on your own terms. God did not choose to make many roads to himself. He chose that 'there is none other name under heaven given among men, whereby we must be saved'" (Acts 4:12).

"But that's the trouble. You Christians are so exclusive." That is another accusation Indians make frequently.

"How can you say that?" I countered. "The way is available to every man. Is that being exclusive? Your access to God is just as assured as mine is. Is that being exclusive? Hardly. It is more than generous. God only requires that we come on his terms. I did not make the rules. You are excluding yourself. I am not excluding you.

"Back to that mountain. You know, at the very peak of a mountain there is room for only one road to wind up the last steep incline to the top. It certainly cannot be a broad road. Have you ever seen a cable car? That can more aptly be likened to the way God has provided. It takes a straight, narrow path up the mountainside to the very top. And it has room for only two, Christ and you. It connects to the point where man has gone as far as he can go on his own. Whether or not you get in the car is up to you. You have a free choice. But if you ever reach God you must get in. That is definite. If you get in, your passage is assured. Only as you get in can you look back down the mountainside and see the futility of your former striving."

There was a long, peaceful silence, the kind that comes when words have been exhausted and only silence can express the soul.

"My friend, that is as simple as I can make it," I said, as we parted.

Again the next day he challenged me with, "Christianity is so dogmatic. Hinduism is broad."

"I don't think so." I shook my head and asked, "Is insisting that there are ten paths to God less dogmatic than insisting that there is only one? Is insisting on belief in reincarnation any less dogmatic than saying that there is eternal life in Christ? Hardly. Which man is the more broadminded, he who says that all religions are the same and insists that all men agree with him, or he who says that Christ is the Way and leaves all men free to make their own choice? There is a certain amount of dogma in all truth. Is the inorganic chemist dogmatic because he insists that table salt is sodium chloride?" I laughed. "The answer might be yes and no. He is merely stating a truth proved by experience. It could be a dogma, but in science we call it truth or fact."

For several days, I did not see Mr. Srivastava. I assumed that he was reading or seeking other counsel, or making a religious pilgrimage to famous temples nearby. Like many people in the subcontinent, he had found truth and even recognized it, but commitment meant breaking with his family, his culture, his inheritance. Every root and security he knew in this life had to be severed if he accepted Christ. Thousands throughout the country are in this position today—halfway between belief and commitment.

Mr. Srivastava's quest is a symbol of the quest in the minds of Asians in general, and of all men everywhere. Some are in search of spiritual values, others in search of material or secular things; but all are seeking.

The idea that the East is spiritual and the West material has been thrown by all honest Easterners and Westerners into that barrel know as "false assumption." The ambitions of the average Indian or Pakistani are just as material as those of an American or a European or a Japanese. The prosperity of the West materially has undoubtedly whetted the appetites of Asians for some of the same things, and the search for material values is a tremendous driving force in Asia today, a force they often try to ignore. At least, they hate to admit it.

If one should examine the aims of governments in the subcontinent or in the rest of Asia, he would discover that their ambitions are not different from those of Canada, a European country, or the U.S.A. Every country desires a better life, at least food and shelter, for its people. It is not bad to desire those things.

The Christian and Jewish faiths are the only major religious groups that have come to grips with this question of material things. They recognize that material things are not bad in themselves. Evil comes only with improper stewardship of the material gifts of God. The average Indian still suspects that one who has much in the way of material things cannot be spiritual.

As Christians meet the needs of the hungry, the naked, and the diseased, many people learn that material things can be used for the glory of God. A lesson in action punctuates a thousand sermons.

Many of this generation's university students have fallen victim to secularism. They deny any religious values. Most of them have a material outlook. Rather than antireligious, they are just indifferent—a common trend among students the world over. Contributing to this phenomenon in India and Pakistan is the fact that most students witnessed as children the massacre at the time of the partitioning. This was really a Hindu-Muslim religious war. Some Hindu students point to social abuses in their nation and blame those on religion. They point to colonialism and imperialism and blame them on Christianity or Islam.

Devout religious leaders in the subcontinent look at this indifference to religion with fear and trembling. That may explain why Pakistan is moving toward a more staunchly Muslim state. She fears her people may lose all sense of the religious values the nation was born to protect.

Religious indifference certainly explains the extreme Hindu nationalism that has developed in some parts of India. Some people fear that secular India is selling her soul for material gain. This group finances the military training of their youth to defend their faith. They look forward to establishing a Hindu India. It was a member of this extreme group that assassinated Gandhi. Because he spoke out against many evils in Hindu society, some considered him a traitor rather than a reformer.

Another trend among Hindus in India is that of becoming followers of Gandhi. No single village of any size lacks some kind of statue of him. All villages display his picture. In the railroad stations are pictures of him in sandals and with a walking stick. Underneath are the words, "He showed us the way." Many of his followers have deified him and hung on his every word as the ultimate in truth. Gandhi was much influenced by other than Hindu writings, and especially by the New Testament's Sermon on the Mount, but he was radically opposed to evangelism and conversion. His teachings and his disciplined life have had a lasting impact on Indian thought. Many never look elsewhere for truth.

Down through the centuries, some great problems have arisen in the religious conscience of the subcontinent. Buddhism's attempt to answer them has already been mentioned. At different times other religious groups such as the Jains, Sikhs, and Theosophists have tried to answer some questions arising out of a deep unrest in the soul. Each has receded or else been relegated to a sect because it provided no final answers.

When Mr. Srivastava suddenly reappeared, just as if he had never been gone, I asked no questions. I learned later, though, that he attended, among other things, a Communist rally and a few Bible classes.

Some people feel that communism has no appeal to the subcontinent, and it is true that Muslims in general reject this atheistic "ism" and are in sympathy with thirty million fellow Muslims who are persecuted in Russia. Others have said that India has nothing to fear from communism.

One man remarked, "Wait until the Indian mind finishes with communism! Peiping will wonder where the *red* went!"

Admittedly, Hinduism engulfed the Dravidian's animism, absorbed and extinguished Buddhism, protected itself from the onslaught of Islam, and practically immunized itself against Christianity. But that does not mean that communism must not be reckoned with.

A large red balloon, several feet in diameter, floated lazily above an office building one day when I was in Madras. The breeze tossed it here and there. Suddenly it twisted a full 180 degrees, displaying a large hammer and sickle on the side. That told the story. Election time was near. Campaigns were hot. The Communists did not expect to win that election, but they were keeping their claims before the people. At almost every crossing, large red banners across the streets carried such slogans as "Liberate India," marked with hammer and sickle.

Many small shops in India fly a red flag outside their entrances. We have gotten over the shock Americans usually feel when they see these flags, but they still remind us that communism is capable of winning the allegiance of the subcontinent.

Communism in India and Pakistan receives greatest support in the "enlightened" south where the percentage of Christians is highest; in the labor unions, in the city slums, in areas of poverty and famine, it scored few triumphs. Why? One would expect the opposite.

This has happened because communism has made a dynamic appeal to many intellectuals. Erroneously, it has been called the greatest brotherhood ever offered to the subcontinent. Many men, Lalitha's father, for example, have cut across every precept of Hindu society to meet the demands of total obedience to the party. Communists never campaign in the subcontinent against religion or any of the other deep-seated cultural traditions. The party's slogan is patriotism.

Communists are opportunists. They involve themselves in the struggles of the common man, setting up communism as the panacea for all ills. Whether attacking the landlords, the industrial magnates, or the moneylenders, their purpose is always consistent. They want to appeal to the masses and gain financial support for the party.

The Communist party has literally flooded India and Pakistan with attractive literature at giveaway prices. Millions of idle people have nothing better to do than read it. Yet, Mr. Srivastava had to catch a bus and ride fifty miles to buy a New Testament hidden beneath the counter!

Even though communism poses as the downtrodden man's deliverer, a close scrutiny of the party in the subcontinent reveals empty promises. Communists have trained people to make bombs and sabotage trains, but they have never organized a school for the poor. They have sheltered striking laborers, but have never built shelters for any orphans. They claim to be the hope of the hungry peasant, but during times of famine they have not rushed to bring relief. Their record in ministering to the suffering or establishing hospitals for the sick is blank.

With this record, why do they continue to win so many Asians? Could it be because they are unrelenting in demanding total self-sacrifice and unwavering devotion? In these qualities, they far surpass what the majority of Christians have done for their faith.

There is a bright side. The Communist government of the state of Kerala has been replaced. China's annexation of Tibet and attack on the Indian border have caused many people to take a more sober look at the inside of communism. The Communist party has called attention to many ills in the social structure of the subcontinent, and the present democratic governments, which are also aware of these problems, are diligently trying to correct them. As one compares the progress of the subcontinent against that of mainland China in the midst of the same intense revolution, there is comfort in thinking that the evidence against communism will speak for itself.

But will it? Can all people or even enough people be sufficiently objective to weigh all of the evidence?

Today's battlefield is no longer a Normandy or a Bunker Hill or a Guadalcanal. Today's warfare is raging within the minds of men, and even though by present-day standards these battles appear more civilized, their ultimate goal is the same—to kill. Which is worse, to devour a man's body or his soul? In the midst of Asia's current revolution, a powerful and subtle psychological warfare is being waged. The prize of victory is man's total allegiance.

This is not the subcontinent's first encounter with clever mental maneuvering. Along the trails of Khyber Pass, the western gate to the subcontinent, have come for centuries not only invading armies, but engulfing, peaceful, and subduing ideologies. As seen in the previous chapter, suave Brahmans before the Christian era learned the cunning of surrounding themselves with a theology that placed them in physical, spiritual, political, and economic control of a vast horde of people.

Paralleling what Kenneth Scott Latourette, Baptist historian, said about China, it can be said today that the subcontinent in the past three decades has undergone as much change as Europe has in the last five centuries.

In the midst of this cultural crisis, most of the people are examining new things and ideas and reexamining critically whatever they previously valued.

The battle rages. What are the signposts? Who will show the way? The battle will not be won with gifts from Wall Street, nor with technicians from Moscow. It will be won, village by village, where ordinary friendship overflows the needs of common peoples whom God loves with his total material providence, intellectual wonder, and spiritual reconciliation. God goes to those villages on our feet. He speaks to them with our lips. He lifts them with our hands. He loves them with our hearts. But where are we?

On the day he talked to me after returning from the Communist rally, Mr. Srivastava suddenly blurted, "Don't both Christianity and communism offer brotherhood?" His question is being asked by many.

I pondered a while before answering: "But only Christianity offers sonship. There can be no true brotherhood apart from sonship. Before we can become brothers, we must first become sons of God. That is possible only in Christ." Laughingly, I added, "My friend, how many of the answers you already know, I am not sure. But of one thing I am sure. You know all the questions! I think we need to go back to the foot of that mountain. The cable car is waiting there!"

Mr. Srivastava looked at me wearily. "I thought those roads led up the mountain, but that was an illusion. They went up a little, then curved around the side and down into a spiritual Sahara. My soul is parched." He moistened his lips as he spoke.

I continued, "Listen again, as Jesus says, 'If any man thirst.'"

This was the search of only one man's soul. There are millions of others who seek, but few of them have guides.

# 3 Christ Comes to the Subcontinent

The *Kron Princess Maria* set sail from Dover. The year was 1793. As passengers William Carey and his family stepped ashore in Calcutta, India, the present-day missionary movement was on its way. Surely, the Danes did not know that their ship was launching modern missions.

Any of a hundred books on missions could begin with similar statements. But they do not speak the whole truth. They are certainly inadequate as an account of the Christian witness beneath the Himalayas, and they give the erroneous impression that for eighteen hundred years God was without a witness among the Hindus and Muslims of the subcontinent. The fact is that, in addition to "the true Light, which lighteth every man," God has from early times sent out witnesses to the land of the Indus. Esther 1:1 mentions India.

There is much to support belief that the apostle Thomas preached in India in the first century. He probably preached to the Hebrew community in Cochin. People there were expecting a Messiah; he was bringing the good news. He reputedly founded churches in what is now the state of Kerala, and there is a monument in the city of Madras where he was supposedly martyred for preaching Christ. This is quite possibly true, but the history is unrecorded.

It is a matter of historical record that there were Christian churches in India in the last part of the second century when the philosopher Pantaenus visited the subcontinent. After his conversion from Stoicism, he became Christianity's most able scholar of his age and is history's earliest recorded missionary to India. Jerome, author of the Latin Vulgate version of the Bible, recorded in the fourth century that Pantaenus was sent to India "to preach Christ among the Brahmans." On arriving in India, Pantaenus found a small, thriving group of Christians and brought back an early edition of the Gospel of Matthew from India to Egypt. This is factual evidence of an earlier witness in India.

Very little is recorded of this early period, and many men less well-known than Pantaenus may have preached in India. One historian reports that when Constantine, emperor of Rome, called the first church Council of Nicea in A.D. 325, a "bishop of India" was present.[1]

Down through the centuries God has used persecution to scatter his people with his message. In the early fifth century, a large group of Christians led by Nestorius, the archbishop of Constantinople, revolted against calling Mary the "Mother of God." Nestorius and his followers were driven into exile and severely persecuted. As a result, they scattered over all of the known world, preaching as they went. From this group two major arms of missionary effort developed. One reached across to China and Mongolia; the other moved into South India. In India the Nestorians found a good-sized body of Christians with whom they united. A very strong and faithful group in the fifth century, they were willing

[1]Lemuel Call Barnes, *Two Thousand Years of Missions Before Carey* (Chicago: Christian Culture Press, 1900), p. 89.

to suffer martyrdom for their faith. During this period of advance of the gospel, old manuscripts record sixteen thousand names of clergy martyred in India in the short span of thirty-five years. Thousands of less prominent people undoubtedly were slaughtered also. It was an age-old lesson. The church becomes stronger and even multiplies in the face of the bitterest persecution.

The Syrian Orthodox Christians of Kerala today hold to the belief that they are "St. Thomas churches." Originally, Christians from Syria may have come to India to escape persecution in their own country in the first century, or they may have been won to Christianity by the preaching of the apostle Thomas after they came to India. Unfortunately, these details are unrecorded in history. It is possible that the Christian churches existing in India in the fifth century were engulfed by the Syrian Nestorian churches. Until recently, bishops of the Syrian Orthodox Church, even though Indian-born, had to go to Antioch, Syria, for ordination.

Although these groups were known in the early period for evangelizing the people around them, they later became an ingrown body of Christians with no outreach. Many of today's evangelical bodies tend to be highly critical because Syrian Orthodox Christians have not evangelized India in these two thousand years. They might be less critical if they looked back at the history of the fourth to eighth centuries when there were mass murders of Christians. As a matter of survival in a hostile society Christians tended to build a shell around themselves. It is not the building of the shell, but the maintenance of it for centuries that goes unjustified. Today there is a new vitality and evangelistic concern, and in many areas the old shell has crumbled.

About seventy-five years ago, a stirring in the Syrian Orthodox churches resulted in the breaking away of a number of these Christians to form the Mar Thoma (Saint Thomas) churches. This group has put away such practices as worship of the virgin Mary and praying for the dead.

The founder of the Mar Thoma group, Abraham Malpan, is called the "Luther of Travancore" (TRAVan-kohr, now the state of Kerala). Like Martin Luther in the German Reformation, he stopped short of a total reformation to biblical Christianity. For that reason, new attempts at reformation have arisen from time to time. Recently a group of about fifty thousand people broke off from the Mar Thoma churches to form the St. Thomas Evangelical churches.

Today the combined membership of the Syrian Orthodox, the Mar Thoma, and the St. Thomas Evangelical churches is approximately one million. There have never been any Western missionaries or financial support to these groups. They themselves have missionaries throughout India and in several Asian countries.

In many ways these evangelical branches of the Eastern church are in the best position to win India to Christ. First of all, they are Indians. Next, they have the intellect, the educational background, the leaders, and the finances to do it. They are a highly respected group in Indian society. Many of them hold top government posts throughout the country. We should sincerely pray for a moving of the Holy Spirit in their churches so that they may reap the harvest at their fingertips.

Vasco da Gama took Catholicism to India in 1498 under the Portuguese flag. It is worth a chuckle to note that the first Catholic converts were of the fisherman caste. In the mid-sixteenth century Francis Xavier, a Spanish Jesuit, sailed on a Portuguese ship from Lisbon to Goa on the west coast of India. Although his work was short and shallow, he is still revered by Catholics in India. The Catholics were entrenched in Goa under the protection of the Portuguese army. As they went southward, they came in conflict with the Syrian Orthodox churches of South India and so severely persecuted them that by the close of the eighteenth century only 116 of the previous 1,400 Orthodox churches remained. Of these, 84 united with the Roman Church under pressure. Only 32 struggling Syrian Orthodox churches remained.

Despite the black marks on her advance, the Roman Catholic Church has had many dedicated missionaries in India. They have contributed a great deal in the field of education. Today, Catholics make up about 50 percent of those who claim to be Christians in India. Their total membership is about 5,000,000. However, the Protestant community is larger, actually, because many Protestant groups count only members who have professed faith, while Catholics count whole families, including infants, who have been baptized.

The current trend in India is for church union. In 1947, the Congregational, Presbyterian, Anglican, and Methodist denominations in the south united to form the Church of South India. Currently, conferences between Roman Catholics and the Church of South India are being held to discuss union. The average member of the Church of South India is not involved in the discussions. In fact, he is hardly aware of the issues involved, since the union movement is taking place at the leadership level. Many on the local scene feel that the Roman Catholic Church may see in the Protestant ecumenical movement an opportunity to gather most of the branches of Christendom back into its fold. It seems likely that if a union between the Church of South India and the Roman Catholic Church ever occurs, it will be on the terms of the latter.

European Protestants first sent missionaries to India in 1705. The missionaries were two Germans named Bartholomew Ziegenbalg and Henry Plutschau who were sent out by the king of Denmark. They found that Roman Catholics, although they had been there two centuries, had not translated the Scriptures into even one Indian language. The Orthodox churches were still using the Syriac ritual. Since few Indians knew the foreign tongues, their Christian worship was blind. The Protestant missionaries' first task was to master the Tamil language of South India. In 1711, their Tamil New Testament translation was ready. Subsequently, the first book ever printed in India was the Tamil Bible.

In general, the East India trading companies of the various European countries were opposed to Christian mission work. They seemed to fear that their source of cheap labor would be destroyed if the Indians were aroused to their rights as human beings. They feared that the Indians would learn that all men are equal before God. Instructed Indians might hold the Europeans to rules of Christian ethics. Their fears were justified, for Christianity, when taken seriously and completely, shakes society to its foundation. It is the world's most powerful revolutionary force. Just as the Baptist message of liberty helped forge America's freedom in 1776, so it contributed to India's independence in 1947.

The two early European missionaries were imprisoned by the Danish governor of India. This awakened such a storm in Europe that the governments began to fear their own countrymen's reactions.

Danish Protestants sent out another German missionary, Christian Friedrich Schwartz. He lived a frugal village life, much like the early disciples of Jesus, and endeared himself to the Indian people. He was so well liked and trusted that even Indian rulers (the maharajas) sought his counsel, and he was called to arbitrate between them and the British government. In that day, when to Indians the mere sight of a white skin meant imperialism, Prince Ali of Mysore (my-SOAR), faced with a decision involving agreement with the British, said of Schwartz, "Send me the Christian. He will not deceive me." Still today there is a living record of the missionary's works, as mouth to mouth the Indian Christians pass the story of his witness.

These few paragraphs give a scanty background of the land that received in 1793 one of the most unusual men the subcontinent had ever seen—William Carey.

Born in Paulerspury, England, the son of a weaver, Carey showed an early liking for education. In order to pursue his studies, he went to a nearby town as a cobbler's apprentice. It was there that he developed into an independent thinker. Discussing the practices and policies of the Church of England, he and a fellow apprentice could not reconcile them with the teachings of the Bible. The Church labeled the men "dissenters."

Carey became convinced of the Baptist position. In England at that time no one became a Baptist without deep conviction and a willingness to withstand all kinds of persecution. The journal of a Dr. Ryland of Northampton on October 5, 1783, reads, "This day baptized a poor journeyman shoemaker." Today, few people would ever know of Ryland if it were not for William Carey.

After baptism, Carey was licensed to preach. He continued to mend shoes, but his most absorbing avocation was learning. He mastered Greek, Hebrew, Latin, French, and Dutch. He read and reread the appeals of the missionaries, and was moved to action. The writings of Schwartz particularly stirred him to consider his personal obligation to service across the seas.

The Baptist church in Moulton, near London, ordained him, and as its pastor Carey preached of a lost world in need of the good news. Even Dr. Ryland is reported to have rebuked him for his wild ideas, making a statement to the effect that when God got ready to save the heathen, he would do it without the help of Carey or Ryland.

At the next associational meeting, Carey chose Isaiah 54:2-3 for his text, charging his listeners to "expect great things from God, attempt great things for God." The formation of "The Particular Baptist Missionary Society for the Propagation of the Gospel among the Heathen" was accomplished in the parlor of a woman called "Widow Wallis." A collection was taken. That proves it was a Baptist meeting! With just a little over thirteen pounds in the treasury, the march was on. Within a year, Carey sailed with his family for Calcutta in northeast India. Their passage was on a Danish ship because the British government, and especially the British East India Company, was opposed to missionary work.

During his first six years in India, Carey was superintendent of an indigo factory in Calcutta, but he found time to translate the Bible into Bengali (ben-GAHL-ey). Then, forced by the British to leave their territory, he found the Danes at Serampore more friendly.

Serampore was to become the center of British Baptist work in India and an educational center for Indian Christians and intellectuals. Carey's contributions to secular and religious life there were phenomenal. To guide them in their relationships with the Indian people, he and his colleagues in 1805 wrote the Serampore Covenant:

To set an infinite value on the individual soul.
To esteem and treat Indians always as our equals.
To abstain from whatever deepens India's prejudice.
To engage in every work that is for India's good.
To be instant in the nurture of personal religion.
To give ourselves without reserve to the Cause,
    not counting even the clothes we wear our own.

With that spirit William Carey, the intellectual and spiritual giant, translated the whole Bible into six languages, the New Testament into twenty-three, and portions of the Scriptures into ten others. As if that were not enough, he supported himself and his colleagues by his work in the indigo and jute industries. He published the first vernacular newspaper in India. It survives today as the highly regarded *Statesman*. He brought the first steam engine to India. He began education there for women and girls. He started the first organization to improve the country's agriculture. He was the first translator of the Sanskrit classics into English. He began the first medical mission in the land. He awakened America to the cause of missions.

It was Carey who inspired Adoniram Judson and Luther Rice by his vivid descriptions of spiritual darkness in Asia. When a thunderstorm drove five college students under a haystack in Massachusetts in 1806, they debated their personal responsibilities to the area of the world where he served. Then they pledged themselves in prayer for the task. A brotherhood was formed to pray regularly for the lost in the Orient. As proof that one cannot regularly and sincerely pray about a need without doing something about it, Judson and Rice, two of the brotherhood of students, sailed for India to help in the task of evangelization. They were supported by the Congregational churches in America.

During their separate voyages, they studied the Scriptures earnestly. In sincerity and open-mindedness they examined the New Testament teachings, and this led them to the Baptist position. In India they were immersed, thus cutting themselves off from their supporting body in America.

The British Government deported Judson and his wife to Burma, where one of the largest Baptist groups in Asia has developed as an outgrowth of their work. God used unusual circumstances to guide the Judsons into accomplishing his purpose.

Rice returned to the United States to gather support for himself and the Judsons. But he was never able to fulfil his longing to return to India. He was, however, destined to perform one of the most strategic and probably the least appreciated task in Baptist history. Few Southern Baptists realize that their own present mission structures owe their foundations to Luther Rice. Few have faced the fact that Southern Baptists tarried more than a century before recapturing his vision of carrying the gospel to India.

The organization that sent Carey to India became the British Baptist Missionary Society, which has in modern India 122 missionaries working with scores of national

Christian leaders. There are 616 churches with a baptized membership of 46,000 and a total church community of over 100,000. Some of Carey's work was done and is being continued in East Bengal, which is now East Pakistan.

Carey not only brought enlightenment to what are now India and Pakistan, but also to his British homeland. The British rulers in India moved toward social reform and better government policies. Such Indian customs as child sacrifices, child marriages, and the burning of widows on their husband's funeral pyres were outlawed. For the first time, Christians were allowed to hold office in the Indian government service. A bandit gang known as "the Thugs," famous for robbing and then strangling victims with a turban, was extinguished. These and other reforms came into effect in India as the result of an enlightened government, the preaching of the Christian message, and the efforts of Indian reformers.

At an opportune time Baptists of America, whose efforts had been thwarted with the deporting of Judson, were able to open three new mission areas in India. The year was 1836, and Baptists in the United States were still nine years from their division into northern and southern conventions. For that brief period Baptists from the southern states had the opportunity to participate, to some extent at least, in mission endeavors in India.

The mission work of Baptists of America was divided into Assam, Bengal-Orissa, and South India fields. These were so different in language, custom, race, and climate that they could have been in three separate worlds. There was the beautiful, rich, and highly developed Sanskrit language and the dialects of some hill tribes with vocabularies of less than a thousand words. There was the highly educated Brahman and the primitive jungle man without a written alphabet. There were the slightly oriental Assamese, the Bengalese and Telugu of Dravidian origin, and the Aryan races to work among. There were the spirit-worshiping animists, the monotheistic Muslims, the polytheistic Hindus, and a remnant of Buddhists to reach. There were the scorching 120-degree summers on the plains and the below-freezing seasons in the Himalaya Mountains to weather.

The struggles, setbacks, triumphs, and survival of Baptist work under these difficult and varied conditions make thrilling reading in the annals of mission history. Only God could have sustained the missionaries and their work. There are many missionary graves of men, women, and children in India, and yet, one involved in this endeavor wrote, "Happy lot to live in these days."

In 1853, the American Baptist board voted for the second time to close the South India field. Seventeen years of labor had brought only three converts. No one was in training to go to this field, and missionaries who had been there were on furlough in broken health. On the mission map of South India was a single star. It marked the little mission station in Nellore (neh-LOHR). Dr. Samuel Francis Smith, author of "My Country, 'Tis of Thee," was at a meeting when the vote was taken to close the mission. Catching the poetic magic of the one star on the map, he penned these lines:

> Shine on, "Lone Star"! till earth redeemed
>   In dust shall bid its idols fall;
> And thousands, where thy radiance beamed,
>   Shall "crown the Savior, Lord of all."

The next day, his words were read to the assemblage,

and the struggling little mission was saved. But that was
not its last dark day. Another time it was almost closed,
when one of its missionaries declared that he would return, live, and if required, die among his beloved Telugu.
American Baptists did not realize then that they were on
the verge of a phenomenal ingathering of God's chosen
ones. But God did.

Today, one of the strongest, ablest, and largest single
language groups of Baptists in all of Asia lives in that
area. In the three fields of India where American Baptists work there are approximately 2,700 churches with a
baptized membership of nearly 350,000. They operate
numerous schools and several hospitals, help support
several colleges and institutions of higher learning, and
carry on an active evangelistic program.

The second largest theological seminary in India is the
Ramapatnam Baptist Theological Seminary in Telugu
country. Its president is Dr. Maurice Blanchard, a Southern Baptist of Chattanooga, Tennessee, who felt God
calling him to India. Appointed by the American Baptist
board in 1941, he and his family have greatly enriched
the Christian witness in South India. The Blanchards
and Mr. and Mrs. Mike Ray, who served in the South
India field eleven years, are typical of many Southern
Baptists who felt God's call to India and were true to
the call in spite of the fact that Southern Baptists had
no mission work in the subcontinent.

Canadian Baptists have a thriving work in India. In
fact, Samuel Day, the founder of the "Lone Star Mission" of American Baptists, was a Canadian. At the time
he went to India, the Baptists of Canada did not have
their own separate mission board.

A telegraph operator from many miles north of the

Missionaries Jasper L. and Dorothy McPhail
with Miss Kathleen Cutshaw, director of the language school,
United Theological College, Bangalore, India

Dr. Gwenda Lewis (Welsh, British Baptist),
professor of anesthetics, and Dr. George P. Varkey,
a graduate trainee, in the anesthesia department
of Christian Medical College Hospital
in Vellore, India

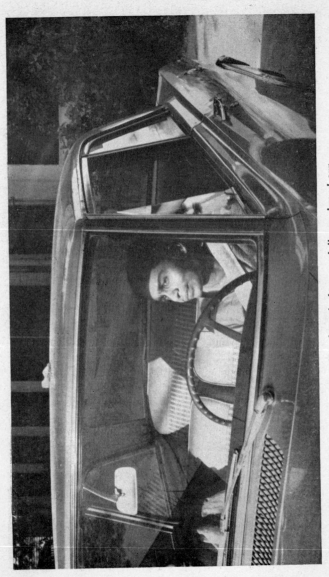

Dr. Mary Verghese in her specially-equipped car
at Christian Medical Hospital
in Vellore, India

*Hindu temple in Vellore, India*

Carey family tomb in College graveyard
at Serampore, India

Laborers on a business street in Feni,
East Pakistan

Conference of surgeons at Christian
Medical College Hospital, Vellore, India;
Dr. McPhail is below the window

Photographs by Fon H. Scofield

"Lone Star Mission" was converted while working in the town of Nellore. When he went back to his hometown of Kakinada (cock-uh-NAH-dah), he resigned his job and gave himself to the preaching of the gospel. Soon a church of 150 members was gathered, and the preacher began to look for a mission society to help build his work. Canadian Baptists, deciding to organize their own board, undertook to develop the work at Kakinada in northern Andhra, a Telugu-speaking area.

They had a mature work almost from the beginning. In the year 1878, ten thousand Telugus were baptized in the Canadian and American Baptist fields. What an encouragement to the four-year-old Canadian Mission!

Educational and medical work have gone hand in hand with the development of the evangelistic witness. High schools, training schools, literacy work, seven hospitals, two leprosaria, several dispensaries, and a number of orphanages have been used in conjunction with the setting up of New Testament churches to minister to the whole man. The missions have fostered in churches and institutions the development of strong leadership among the nationals, who have excelled especially in village evangelistic and medical work.

Canadian Baptists operate a theological college in Kakinada and also train Indian women in Bible work. In addition to work among the Telugu, they have growing work with others at the northern edge of their field.

About seventy Canadian missionaries work along with many national workers in all their mission locations in South India. More than 165 churches with a baptized membership of nearly forty thousand comprise the "Northern Circars" (SIR-cars), the name of the convention of these Baptists in the state of Andhra.

Most of the work of Australian Baptists in the subcontinent is situated in East Pakistan. During recent years they have begun work in Assam, the northeastern province of India. Working in some very primitive areas, they have utilized small dispensaries, union farming co-operatives, village schools, a high school, and infant- and maternal-care services to undergird their program of evangelism.

There are countless examples of how God has used humble beginnings and dedicated workers to make a people for himself where there was none before.

Dr. Zok Muana, an intern in the Christian hospital of Vellore, South India, came from the hills of Tripura. His parents are humble folk who responded to the gospel when it was brought to their village by New Zealand Baptists. Zok grew up in a home which had a simple reverence for the Bible. However, like many Indian boys, even some Christians, he seemed to think religion was something one inherited from parents.

It was during a two-year battle with tuberculosis as a teen-ager that Zok came to a deep personal faith in Christ. After a long period of Bible study and meditation, he dedicated himself to the Christian witness through a ministry of medical evangelism. His preparation has been completed, and he has returned to his home as a medical doctor bearing his witness for Christ.

As he returned to his village, his parents, his fellow villagers, and his supporting mission all awaited him in keen anticipation. The first among them to have studied medicine, he is their symbol of a new day for his people. What if New Zealand Baptists had not gone to Tripura?

Mr. S. J. Dawson is professor of Tamil language at Union Theological College, maintained in Bangalore by the Church of South India. When he was a young man, he and his family were devotees of Shiva, one of the Hindu gods. High-caste people with religious insight and depth, they sought the true and living God in the only way they knew, through rituals and sacrifices.

A group called the Strict Baptists of England began mission work in their area. Under the power of the gospel, the inadequacy of the family faith was revealed, and the carnality of Shaivism became repulsive to them. The entire family came into the Christian fold. For many years the older Mr. Dawson was a pastor and leader among the Tamil Baptist churches. Now his son is preaching through many lips as he teaches missionaries of all denominations the difficult Tamil language.

But Mr. Dawson does much more than teach Tamil. He and his friend, Mr. Eliah Rao (EL-le-yah row), a Baptist who is professor of Telugu at the same school, spend endless hours taking the gospel message to scattered Tamil and Telugu communities throughout the city of Bangalore. Candidates for baptism are given a course of instruction for six months, and twice a year about thirty new believers are baptized. The two Baptist preachers support themselves by teaching, but their lives are centered in sharing their faith. Thank God that Strict Baptists of England went to India.

The Conservative Baptists of America have work in India and West Pakistan. They operate the Central India Baptist Hospital in Ellichpur (EL-ich-poor) in the same state as Bombay. Short of personnel and badly overworked, the one doctor and two nurses there seem to be meeting a tremendous need in a gallant but tiring work. The doctor is Dr. Morris Powell, a graduate of North Carolina Baptists' Bowman Gray School of Medicine.

Of particular interest to Southern Baptists is the work of Baptist Mid-Missions in Assam, because Dr. and Mrs. Gene Burrows serve in this field. Gene is a 1954 graduate of Baylor University College of Medicine in Houston, Texas, having previously graduated from Texas Baptists' Howard Payne College in Brownwood. His wife Bette is a graduate also of Howard Payne and of the Lillie Jolly School of Nursing at Baptist Memorial Hospital in Houston, Texas. This young couple is well known to many Southern Baptists.

India was not new to Gene Burrows. His father and mother went to Alipur (ah-le-POOR), Assam, in January, 1940. His father, a doctor, died on his first furlough back in the States, but Gene's mother returned to India with her small daughter. She left Gene and his younger brother in college in Texas.

It was to the land of his childhood that Gene returned in 1958. He runs a 200-patient leprosy colony in Makunda (mah-COON-dah) and helps with the 65-bed general hospital and the 45-bed tuberculosis hospital at nearby Alipur. Bette teaches in the nursing school, teaches Bible courses, and cares for their five children.

The Baptist Mid-Missions group is one of the warmest and most fervent in India. From a meager beginning in 1936, its missionary staff has grown to twenty-six. With a burden to see the unevangelized reached with the message of salvation, this growing mission is the light of Christ on the horizon for two million Indians in one small portion of Assam.

The Swedish Baptists of America, now known as General Conference Baptists, work in the area adjoining the North Eastern Frontier Area (NEFA) where the Chinese attacked in 1962. For many years they worked in Assam under the American Baptist Foreign Mission Societies. A few years ago the conference organized its own foreign mission board, and its missionaries were given the northernmost area of the Assam field.

During the 1962 border conflict between China and India, these missionaries and their Indian colleagues ministered to many refugees. Also, the local people became more responsive to the gospel. Later, when foreigners in the territory were evacuated to Calcutta, news of the evacuation failed to reach three of the single women until very late because they were too near the enemy. They packed up and set out in an old car without a clutch. The Lord delivered them as they drove through fifty miles of military maneuverings just hours before escape would have been completely cut off.

Their story was told me while I was treating one of them in Vellore. Her two companions added their bit of intrigue to the story. I thought: Those women have been scared within an inch of their lives; they'll never return to NEFA. A few weeks later, word came that the area was opened up again to foreigners, and I learned that the three women were among the first to return to their posts of duty.

"I did not want to leave in the first place," Arlene Peterson said. "What did my fellow Indian Christians think of me, running out on them at a time like that? They had to stay there, but I had to obey government orders!"

God sometimes places his followers in dangerous places to bear witness. In crisis hours, he thrusts them into the thick of the situation, just as he placed those three missionaries. He does not always guarantee safety. Southern Baptists' own Bill Wallace of China is an example. But God does guarantee security, and eternity will reveal it. Bill Wallace is eternally secure in the arms of the Father who called him to this life and to martyrdom. Lesser men and women count the cost and retreat —retreat to nurse their nimble souls while the gospel witness recedes before the avalanche of a godless creed.

All together, about twenty-five different Baptist and Baptist-like missions are working in India. There are about one and a half million Baptist church members there—the largest group in any free country other than the United States. (Although Russia reports 2,000,000 Baptists, this may well be for world propaganda purposes. The accepted figure is 550,000.) The vitality of Baptist groups in India could well mean that they are on the brink of a great advance. This advance could begin with relatively few but strategic modifications.

First of all, regional, language, and racial loyalties keep members of the various groups from thinking of themselves as Indian Baptists. They are not organized and united as a group. Too often they think of themselves as "Telugu Baptists" or "Assam Baptists." I met a young Baptist leader one day who introduced himself by saying, "I am a Canadian Baptist." Jesting, I replied, "For a minute I was mistaken. I would have guessed you were an Indian!" They need to think of themselves as Indian Baptists instead of as satellites of Canadian or American Baptist churches.

Next, like Baptists everywhere, they need to know the Scriptures better. They have learned to cooperate across denominational lines in such matters as literature, student work, evangelistic campaigns, and Christian education. This, as such, is good. But often it has been at the cost of compromise or a watering down of scriptural teachings. Fidelity to the Scriptures has been distinctive of Baptists down through the centuries. Wherever they have departed from that principle, they have lost their unique and most powerful witness in the building of New Testament churches. Many Indian Baptists are educated in union Christian colleges or union seminaries which are dominated by liberal or Anglican theology. Baptist educational institutions in India need strengthening.

The largest single non-Catholic denomination in India is the Baptist group. With their resources, with good leadership and unity, and with the power of the Holy Spirit, Baptists could change India in the next generation. Oh, for an Indian Luther Rice to lead them!

Almost every denomination in Europe and North America has mission work in India. Disregarding the now-closed China mission field, the nation probably has had more mission effort poured into it than any other in the world. There have been Christian missionaries in almost every town of any size in the land, and especially in the south. Yet Christianity has touched but a fraction of India's 450,000,000 people, because most of them live in rural villages.

With the population increasing at the rate of eight to ten million every year, many missions are finding it difficult to maintain the status quo in India, and there are fewer Protestant missionaries there now (about three thousand) than in 1920 (over five thousand). The drop in number of missionaries is partly due to the government's policy of admitting very few missionaries for evangelistic work now. Almost all new visas are being given only to those with training in special technological, medical, or sociological fields. More and more of the work of evangelism is falling on Indian shoulders.

The Christian medical colleges and hospitals in Vellore (Madras state), South India, and Ludhiana (loo-dy-AH-nah, in Punjab), North India, represent the combined efforts of many missions in India. It is at the medical center in Vellore, begun by Ida Scudder early in this century, that Southern Baptists' first representatives in India were stationed.

A granddaughter of the first American medical missionary in India, young Ida S. Scudder was gay and high-spirited. Reared in South India, she had already made up her mind that a missionary's life was not for her. She enjoyed the social life of one of the better eastern schools in the United States and preferred to remain there.

When word came that her mother was severely ill and that she was needed back in India to help the family, she returned. But in Ida's mind it was only a temporary return.

She had been in America so long that she had forgotten what India was like. Life seemed quaint. The clack-clack of ox carts along the road outside her room at night, the weird music that pierced the air, the cow-dung odors that were so permeating, the filth that poverty breeds—all reminded her of her desire to get back to America. But God had a plan.

After dark one evening, young Ida answered a knock on Dr. Scudder's door. There stood a village man who told his story. His young wife could not deliver their baby. The village women had tried all their concoctions to no avail. As a last resort, he had come to the missionary. Miss Scudder explained that she was not a doctor, but that her father would be glad to help. The village man shook his head. It was against their custom. No man ever was allowed to minister, even as a doctor, to the village women. The man walked away into the night.

Before long there was another rap at the door and Ida answered it. Another man with an identical story was there. Again Ida said that her father would help. With the same hopeless expression, the second man refused and walked away.

Ida returned to her reading, but was soon disturbed by a knocking at the door. Another villager with the same plea faced her. The same offer. The same refusal. The same fallen countenance. These men needed a woman doctor to care for their womenfolk.

Miss Scudder went to bed, but not to sleep. She tossed and turned. The next morning, three funeral processions passed through the village. Three Indian village women had sought help, but none suitable to their quaint customs could be found. They and their unborn babies were on their way to the funeral pyre. Death to them was better than to break custom.

Ida Scudder realized her individual responsibility before God. She fell on her knees, and when she arose she had committed herself to God and to India.

She could hardly wait to get back to America—the same desire, a different motive. She studied medicine and went back to India. It was 1900. The task before her was impossible. She could not care for all of the women in South India.

The vision came to her of training Indian women to care for their own people. By doing that she could multiply her effectiveness. First, she began a nursing school in Vellore. Then, in 1918, she started a class of girls in the study of medicine. People laughed at her. How could one doctor, a woman at that, teach all of the subjects in medical school? No one yet knows the answer, but those who laughed had to laugh at themselves. When those girls appeared for the Madras state examination several years later, all of them passed.

No woman in South India today need die unnecessarily in childbirth for lack of women doctors. This is due largely to the work and influence of Ida Scudder. The needs of a growing medical school caused her to seek help outside her own Reformed Church in America. She began to enlist finances, personnel, and prayers from many other denominations, agencies, and other groups. About sixty different groups from all over the world contribute toward the work.

In 1942, the school was upgraded, and the first male students were admitted in 1947. The central unit is an 850-bed hospital. The nursing school has both the diploma course and the course for a bachelor of science degree in nursing. Both groups take midwifery training. Twenty candidates for B.S. degrees and forty-five for diplomas are admitted each year. Also twenty-five postgraduate nurses are trained each year in teaching, public health, or nursing administration. The medical college admits sixty students each year, of whom at least twenty-five are women. In addition, the hospital offers training to over a hundred house surgeons (equivalent to a two-year rotating internship). Specialty training is offered in many branches of medicine. A number of nationals and missionaries go to Vellore for short-term training in special fields without working toward degrees or diplomas, studying only long enough to equip themselves to meet the needs in their local situations.

With the motto, "Not to be ministered unto, but to minister," the institution has grown into one of the most highly respected medical centers in all Asia. It sets the standards in many fields in India and has very good rapport with the Indian government.

Dr. Jacob Chandy, the principal of the medical school, was the first neurosurgeon in India, and the first department of neurosurgery in India was developed at Vellore. It is now the all-India training center in that field and trains even government-sponsored candidates for the postgraduate degree in neurosurgery. Holding advisory posts in the World Health Organization (WHO), Dr. Chandy is internationally known, and was decorated by the government of India for service to the country. He is one of many outstanding Indians at Vellore.

For many years, Baptists have played a part in the ministry of the Vellore institutions. Dr. Carol Jameson, recently retired as professor of obstetrics and gynecology, was an American Baptist. Dr. and Mrs. Wayne Gordon, also American Baptists, served for a time in the department of medicine before retiring to Lexington, Kentucky. Mr. and Mrs. Howard Stalker, American Baptists from Ohio, gave two of their postretirement years to helping with the building and engineering problems of the college and hospital. Dr. and Mrs. John S. Carman, American Baptists who have been in India since 1928, have long been leaders at Vellore. Formerly professor of surgery and urology, Dr. Carman is now the director. Mrs. Carman was until recently the treasurer. Their son Robert, a clinical pathologist, and his family are in Vellore also. Dr. Leroy Allen, now head of the Indian branch of the Rockefeller Foundation in Delhi, was formerly under appointment of American Baptists as professor of public health at Vellore. Dr. Harold Thomas, formerly an American Baptist missionary to China,

now in his late seventies, has spent some time in Vellore
to help out during a shortage of radiologists.

Baptists from other countries also work in Vellore. Dr.
Paul Brand, British, internationally known for his development of reconstructive surgery for the hands and feet
of leprosy victims, is a Strict Baptist who was born in
India of missionary parents. For several years he has
worked in close association with Dr. Mary Verghese, who
is the central character of Dorothy Clarke Wilson's book,
*Take My Hands.* Dr. Gwenda Lewis, with the British
Baptists, retired in 1965 as professor of anesthesia. After
coming to India she had polio and is now, like Dr. Verghese, a paraplegic, but she carried on her teaching and
her work from a wheelchair with amazing independence.
Most of her colleagues forgot that she had a handicap.
Miss Eugenia Pranke, a physiotherapist, and Miss Ilene
Greenood, a nurse specialized in leprosy care, are
Canadian Baptists. Miss Elizabeth Carrol, a Scottish Bap-
tist, is a laboratory technologist in charge of the blood
bank.

Including students, faculty, and paramedical workers,
there are about forty Baptists at the medical center in
Vellore.

Dr. Reeve Betts, the first thoracic surgeon in India,
now of Oteen, North Carolina, is a Baptist, but was supported by American Methodists in his work at Vellore.
At the time he began the department there eighteen
years ago, it was the only thoracic center in India. After
twelve years, Dr. Betts returned to the United States.
During that time, he trained thirty Indian thoracic
surgeons. The department cares for all types of chest,
lung, and heart surgery, including open-heart. This is
also the training center for government-sponsored candi-

dates in thoracic surgery. It is in this department that I work, at present as acting head of the department.

Mrs. McPhail and I are the first Southern Baptists to serve in India under the Foreign Mission Board of the Southern Baptist Convention. I am a general and thoracic surgeon. Mrs. McPhail, a nurse anesthetist, works in the Anesthesia Department at the main hospital.

For a number of years Southern Baptists have desired to begin work in India. Several former China missionaries tried to get visas to enter, but were unsuccessful. The doors seemed closed.

When God sends a call, he prepares someone and opens the way. While studying Baptist history, I wondered why no Southern Baptist had caught Luther Rice's vision of India. On several occasions representatives of the Foreign Mission Board discussed with me the problem of getting into India. It would be more realistic to prepare for one of the fields with established work, they suggested.

Repeatedly the frustration of a call and a closed door haunted my mind. For a time, I toyed with the idea of going to India with another mission board. That might have solved my personal problem, but it would not have solved the problem of Southern Baptists as a group. In 1957, I reached a decision. If God were calling me to India, then he must also be calling Southern Baptists. There seemed to be no other denomination whose total plan, purpose, and program coincided with my own views. To no other group could I give unreserved loyalty. I would stay with Southern Baptists.

I felt that the Lord was leading me to specialize in surgery. Convinced that missionary medicine must always be of the very top caliber, I again asked advice about specializing. This was discouraged because it did not fit as well into the overall medical mission work as did general practice. I pondered this. God was leading me as an individual, but I also had deep loyalties and responsibilities to the group. Finally, I came to the decision that I might be completely wrong in my feelings, that I might never find a use for the special training, but regardless of the consequences, I would be true to that which I felt God was leading me to do.

The special training period ended. Appointment time came. The door to India was closed as tightly as ever. My wife had been a BSU summer missionary in Nigeria a few years before. The hospitals there could certainly use us. During the two years before our appointment we decided that we might go to Nigeria.

After we arrived in Richmond for appointment in 1961, my old impression about India became uncomfortably vivid. But the door was closed.

Just before going for appointment, I had given a devotional about "Christ and Closed Doors." My own words came back to haunt me. I had reminded my audience never to forget that Christ's first appearance to his disciples after his resurrection was through a closed door. I had said that Christ had always specialized in penetrating closed doors. Would he now?

The appointment to Nigeria was accepted, but I discussed the problem with the Mission Board. The men there were just as concerned as I about doing God's will. So in mutual confidence, we and the Board opened conversation about India.

We knew about Vellore. The Mission Board did, too. In fact, just a few months before, the Board had received a letter from Vellore, requesting a surgeon. The golden thread of God's leadership now could be seen from the call, through the years of preparation, and in the conversation with the Foreign Mission Board. There were many hurdles to cross, but one by one they were passed.

If I had not specialized, I could not have qualified for the Vellore faculty. If God had not spoken to me again during the appointment services, I would be in Nigeria. There are so many "if's" connected with our being in India that only the Master Planner could have put all of the pieces in place.

The door to India is still substantially closed! But we are on the other side of that closed door. What of the future? We feel secure in trusting the Lord, who specializes in penetrating closed doors. We know he can do it. In fact, the door seems to be opening a bit for Southern Baptists—at least enough for a Baptist hospital and the evangelistic and church planting opportunities it will offer. Tentative government approval has been received, and plans are being developed even now.

Although the crack of an opening to India is only a tiny one, this is no time for anxiety. It should be a time of deep concern and prayer on the part of Southern Baptists for India and for their work there. In the calm and tranquil assurance that this is God's work, all should be alert to recognize new and more effective ways of penetrating closed doors for him.

# 4 The Land of the Pure

How would you like to have the world in a bag? Pakistan does—in more ways than one. In a very literal way that nation "bags" the rest of the world. She produces 75 percent of the world's jute—100 percent of the best quality. Jute is the strong fiber from which burlap, rope, twine, and even some wearable fabrics are made. The rug in your living room may have a jute backing— jute from Pakistan.

No other new country has assumed such international importance as has Pakistan. Born in 1947, carved from the shoulders of the civilization-weary Indo-Pakistan subcontinent, she has rapidly established herself as a world power.

Pakistan is one of the two largest Muslim countries in the world. As a Muslim state, and with West Pakistan bordering the Middle Eastern countries of Iran and Afghanistan, the new nation gives guidance and advice in any questions involving that area of the world. One thousand miles away, East Pakistan, on the border of Southeast Asia, is important in any decision facing that section of the globe.

Pakistan has come to her present status over what a less ingenious people would have considered insurmountable odds. First of all, she is a geographic absurdity. After it became apparent that the subcontinent would be released from British domination, the Muslim minority felt that the only solution to their problems would be a separate Islamic state. It happened that the two Muslim strongholds were on opposite sides of the subcontinent's broad shoulders.

People of the two sections of Pakistan are different in race, language, and culture. The tan West Pakistanis are tall, sturdy people who are likely descendants of Middle Eastern Muslim invaders. The small, dark-skinned East Pakistanis probably descended from Dravidian people. They have had less economic and educational advantages than their countrymen to the west. The uniting force in this diversified society is Islam, the religion of Mohammed.

Not only the people, but the land itself is different. East Pakistan, the size of Arkansas, has 58 percent of the nation's population. With about one thousand people per square mile, it gives foreigners the impression of "standing room only." Richly supplied with water by the main streams and many tributaries of the Ganges and the Brahmaputra (brah-mah-POO-tra) rivers, this eastern section looks like a tropical, jungled Venice. Floods have to be reckoned with often. Between rivers, lush rice paddies and banana groves add to the tropical scene. Seasonal fruits and multicolored trees add beauty.

Texas-sized West Pakistan makes up 85 per cent of the land area of the nation. The coastal provinces are green along the great Indus River. One area has been called "the California of the Orient" because of its fruit orchards and sunny climate. Most of the western country is barren desert, however, and the rich agricultural areas depend on irrigation for refuge from parching heat. The main crop and staple food is wheat.

What would you do if you were the leader of a new country of eighty million people[1] without even paper clips to begin the office work? Mohammed Ali Jinnah, called the "architect of Pakistan," was in that position. Complicating matters, almost seven million destitute Muslims from India fled to Pakistan. In a land where many people are always a little hungry and where scores of people live out their lives on the verge of starvation, the refugees could have sunk the bobbing economy.

To make matters worse, most of the industry and the educational institutions of the subcontinent were in India. There was not a single jute mill in East Pakistan, the home of the jute plant. They were in India. But the discipline of a dauntless people has brought order.

Spurred by the memory of their humiliating loss of power in India, caused by their failure to hold together, the Muslims of Pakistan are willing now to sacrifice personal wishes for the sake of unity. Only in unity do they have freedom. And freedom is sweet against the backdrop of subjugation and hostility in every phase of their life in Hindu-dominated India. Religious tolerance in India proved, in experience, to be tolerance only if one was willing to become a sect or branch of the Hindu philosophy. Those who were unwilling to give up their convictions were tolerated as an oyster tolerates a grain of sand within its shell. She builds a shell around the alien substance, allowing it the right of domain, but only in a circumscribed existence. From behind the cultural walls of their own nation, the Pakistanis are bursting with new life and enthusiasm.

---

[1]Since Pakistan's founding, its population has increased from eighty million to almost one hundred million.

Softened by their own hard experiences, they are building a democratic state that shows signs of tolerance toward non-Muslim minorities. Occasionally, reports leak out to the newspapers of Hindu shops being burned by Muslims or of the properties of Christians being confiscated. The Pakistani Government does not condone such actions. However, it cannot legislate the personal feelings and actions of every citizen.

While both Islam and Hinduism have loudly and long proclaimed doctrines of tolerance toward other groups, their recent actions humiliate their philosophers. Christians in the subcontinent and elsewhere are reminded of their own dark days of the Crusades, the Inquisition, and the Reformation. All of us should be aware that man's basic problem is himself. We must do something about this problem of intolerance before we destroy each other.

The Hindus think the answer lies in education. Wrong actions, it seems to them, are due to ignorance. But even after education, sin is still there. The heart of man is not changed by education.

The Muslim thinks the answer is to unite all men under Islam. History tells him that Islam's downfall in India was due to squabbles and corruptions within the Muslim camp. The heart of man is not changed, however, by unity that is created by a militant physical power.

The Christian with insight and vision realizes that reconciliation comes between man and man only after it has come between man and God. God is reconciling man to himself through Jesus Christ. Man is reconciled with his fellowman only when his heart has been changed by faith in Christ and indwelled by God's Spirit.

Believing that Christ is the answer to problems of individual soul-sickness as well as to problems of international tensions, believing that sooner or later every man must confess that Christ is Lord, and believing that Christ calls people to be ministers of his reconciling power, Southern Baptists began to look into the vast subcontinent.

Stretching out over miles of desert, jungles, plains, mountains, and paddies, it is a challenging region. Walled in on the north by the eternal snows of the Himalaya Mountains and bordered by the Arabian Sea, the Indian Ocean, and the Bay of Bengal, the subcontinent stretches across oil-rich Assam to the western border of China. The area's six hundred million people appear weary with civilization. The few Southern Baptists who visited the subcontinent saw the hopelessness reflected in their sad eyes and were convinced that Christian charity is to be found in a ministry of reconciliation between man and God. In simple terms, this means evangelism. It means changing a man's heart as well as his physical situation. It means instilling hope which, in fruition, will give initiative. Then, whatever the situation, the initiative of hope will work toward changing it while giving peace within.

Pakistan seemed the place to start. She was literally a new child in an old cradle. Eager to win a place among the nations of the world, she opened her arms to all who would help in any way. Before the land was partitioned in 1947 Southern Baptists could not enter the subcontinent, then called India. Ten years later the door was wide open to some of the same territory called by a different name—Pakistan. The name means "holy place" or "land of the pure."

The first Southern Baptist missionaries, Marjorie and Troy Bennett, entered East Pakistan in 1957. They were not the first Baptists in that area, however. The land included in East Pakistan was a part of "Carey's India." The Pakistani people of East Bengal speak the same language as the Bengalis of Serampore (West Bengal), India, Carey's headquarters. Those who can read, read the Bengali Bible that Carey translated.

During the early days of Christian missions, the missionaries were too few to go around. British Baptists worked hard, but the task was beyond their capacity. A few of their retired missionaries went to Australia and began to kindle the fires of evangelism among Baptists there. This created such interest that over eighty years ago Australian Baptists began to help in the missionary task in East Bengal. In those days, Australian Baptists were so few and scattered that they were not even organized into state conventions. It was the beginning of foreign mission work in what is now East Pakistan that united them in one common task and into one national group of Baptists.

At the turn of the century, Australian Baptists were working in Faridpur, Pabna, Orakandi, Rajbari, Sirajganj, Comilla, Mymensingh, and Noakhali areas of East Bengal. The Muslims and high-caste Hindus were unresponsive. Only the Garo tribesmen in the low-lying hills of Mymensingh district showed a readiness to accept the gospel. Today there is a lively, strong Christian fellowship in Garoland.

Because of the unresponsiveness of the East Bengal Muslims and Hindus, Australian Baptists began to concentrate on the responsive areas. Just three months before Pakistan's independence, they began working among people of the Boro tribe in Assam, India. They also strengthened their work with the Garos. Then they opened up new fields in New Guinea, which now is the largest of their fields in terms of the number of missionaries.

These moves depleted their resources and personnel for the difficult Faridpur, Comilla, and Noakhali districts. They had already vacated some of their stations in East Bengal. Australian Baptists began to analyze their problems. At the same time Southern Baptists, having closed their China missions, were eagerly watching for new opportunities for witness in the Orient. For years, mission volunteers with a call to India had been frustrated. Then came correspondence between the Australian Baptist Foreign Mission Board and the Southern Baptist Foreign Mission Board. They agreed that Southern Baptists would assume responsibility for the work in Faridpur and Comilla districts. It was to the Faridpur district that the Troy Bennetts were sent.

They were welcomed to Pakistan by Southern Baptists! That seemed strange to the Bennetts when they reached there as Southern Baptists' first missionaries. But it was true. Christian laymen—the Roy Clouds and the H. P. Smiths of Texas—welcomed them. While working with the Point Four Program the laymen had created good will for their denomination. The Clouds had started a Sunday School in their home, using Southern Baptist literature. Contributions of money from both families went to help spread the gospel in the local areas. They showed their love and concern for the Pakistanis in many ways, although not sent by "a mission" to do so. The help, the fellowship, and the encouragement given by the laymen were of inestimable value to the missionaries who began Southern Baptist work in the subcontinent.

The old city of Dacca has become the Southern Baptist Mission center in East Pakistan. Most of the missionaries spend some time there in orientation and Bengali language study before going to a more permanent station. The Bennetts first lived in Faridpur. Later, they moved to Dacca because it was a better center for Troy's work as treasurer and business manager of the Mission.

Within a few months of the Bennetts' arrival, Jane and Trueman Moore of Arkansas joined them. The Frank Gillhams from Texas also joined the Mission about the same time, but soon had to transfer to another field. Trueman Moore was the first missionary Southern Baptists sent to East Pakistan who could devote his time fully to evangelistic work.

Although Pakistan is a difficult field, Betty and Pat Johnson, who live in Dacca, feel that they are "called to be faithful rather than successful," as he says. He baptized the first converts resulting from our work in East Pakistan. They were two Muslim men who, becoming interested in Christ through the reading room and student center in Dacca, made professions of faith under the preaching of Trueman Moore.

Betty and James F. McKinley, Jr., now serving in Feni, were for a time the only evangelistic missionaries of any denomination in the Comilla town area. Mr. McKinley stimulated some of the sixty Baptist church members of the Comilla area to begin preaching in an adjoining district where over two million people had been without either a missionary or a national pastor. Mr. and Mrs. Troy Bennett later assumed direction of the work in Comilla, with Mr. and Mrs. Wilson Lofland assisting.

An industrial school at Faridpur was transferred to Southern Baptists along with other Australian Baptist work. It is one of the keys by which missionaries maintain contact with young Muslims long enough to penetrate their deep-seated prejudice concerning Christ. Franklin Baugh, who learned in a foreign missions conference at Ridgecrest that laymen are of vital importance in God's plan for missions, was for a time superintendent of the industrial school. He later was transferred to East Africa, and the superintendent now is Carl Ryther.

Begun in 1910 by Australian Baptists as a small weaving school, the institution later began to offer training in engineering and cabinetmaking. The course required three years, and from eighty to one hundred students were there each year. Graduates of this school are now instructors in technical schools throughout India and Pakistan.

The school started accepting government aid during World War II and became a military training institution. In 1948, shortly after independence, the property was seized by the Pakistani Government, and the Australian superintendent was arrested for alleged misappropriation of government properties. Even though he was cleared of the charges, the government took over the school for three years.

Then, Australian Baptists began closing their work there and turning over the responsibilities of evangelism to Southern Baptists of the United States. After leasing the school for a year, Southern Baptists bought it from the Australians in 1962.

The industrial school faces a challenging task. It needs many improvements and much equipment, for which the Mission looks to the gifts of Southern Baptists. Meanwhile, it continues training small classes in engineering and related fields.

The chief aim of the school is bringing young men into contact with the Christian message by daily association with the Christian men who work and teach there. In addition to observing examples of Christian living, the students also hear the preaching of the gospel at the school.

It was Missionary Harold Cummins who, before he and his wife Betty were forced by illness to transfer to another field, established a morning devotional service and evening vespers at the school. Usually the services are conducted by national Christians or the school staff. It is extremely important that they should be. The missionary's life is an example, but people often think his way of life is a result of his nationality. It is hard to get the lesson across that he lives the way he does because of his new life in Christ. Only when the nationals can see the change in the life of one of their own do they begin to understand the true Christian message.

The influence of the industrial school reaches beyond its own classrooms. Staff members go on preaching tours to the villages around Faridpur. These many communities would never have the opportunity of knowing the gospel story if the school were not in Faridpur.

Jeanne and Charles Beckett, a doctor-preacher team, arrived in East Pakistan four years ago. She is the beginning link in plans for a Southern Baptist hospital in the town of Feni. The first Southern Baptist doctor appointed to that country, she was an encouragement to the Mission in matters of illness.

Dr. Ruth Dickerson, a single woman appointed three

years ago, will be able to give all of her time to the hospital work in Feni. Woman doctors are especially needed in Muslim lands where custom forbids Muslim women the attention of male doctors, but male doctors also find plenty of work. Dr. J W Carney, a surgeon, and his wife Virginia were appointed four years ago. They, too, will help develop the medical work in Feni. A nurse, Mavis Pate, was appointed two years ago.

The medical needs of Pakistan are beyond the understanding of the average American. There is only one doctor for every 85,000 people in the nation. That is like having six doctors for the half million people of Memphis, Tennessee. The nursing situation is improving, but in 1961 there were about two hundred professionally trained nurses for the more than fifty million people in East Pakistan. The situation was made more acute when the subcontinent was partitioned, because most of the schools for training doctors and nurses were in India or West Pakistan. East Pakistani students cannot go to the overcrowded schools in India, and it is a thousand miles to West Pakistan. Most of the students cannot go that far away from home, and the schools in West Pakistan are so crowded that they could not be admitted if they went there.

On the priority list for Southern Baptists should be development here of a good hospital and a good school of nursing. But where are the nurses to make it possible? Are they not working somewhere in the United States, heedless to the needs of Pakistan and to what may be God's will for their lives? Living with the suffering in East Pakistan and seeing the need for nurses, one missionary dreamed he addressed a meeting of Baptist nurses in the homeland. This is what he said:

"You would have to take only a small trip around the poorer sections of Dacca or along one of the roads leading out of Comilla, or visit any city in the land, to see an unforgettable picture of disease and pain and need. The multitudes of undernourished children would speak to you. The young mother, coughing with tuberculosis, trying to care for her helpless babies, would tell you volumes. She will be one of ninety thousand in East Pakistan to die this year of the disease, but not before she gives it to one or all of her small children. This is their inheritance. You could be their future.

"If this were not enough, you could see small children covered with tropical ulcers. Many of them develop blood poisoning and die because there is no one to clean the sores and bandage them carefully. Or the victim of leprosy, with only clubs for hands and pegs for feet and perhaps just one huge cavity where his nose used to be, may be the message you need. If you came now, you could be of only minor help to him, but you could change the entire picture for the next generation of leprosy patients.

"If you are callous enough to close your sentiments to all of these, then you force me to take you on one other journey. I am taking you there because I have never met a Baptist nurse whose heart could not be touched by the suffering of childbirth. On the road from Feni is a small village. As we walk along, cries from a mud hut pierce our ears. By the time we reach the hut, only a gasp is heard. Then silence. An old woman stands in the doorway; other women are seated on the floor around a lifeless body. On the abdomen of the corpse are deep hand and rope marks where the village women tried to force an impossible delivery.

"Life for the mother and baby was so near, but yet so far away. It is merely twenty hours by jet to Pakistan. Southern Baptists are only as far away as your commitment to God and his call to this difficult task.

"Since we do not have nurses to send, one of our surest ways of showing the love of Christ to Muslim and Hindu women is not fulfilled. How long they have to wait depends on the Southern Baptist nurses who are seeking God's will for their lives."

That missionary still is awaiting a response.

In a segregated society like that in Pakistan and India, where there is little contact between women and men outside of the home, missionary women are of special importance to the spread of the gospel among Muslim and Hindu women. (Even in church, women sit on one side and men on the other.) Muslim women are not permitted to go to the mosques to worship. Hindu women believe that their husbands are their gods, and that to be truly religious they must worship them. They may also worship the idols in the temples and still be consistent with Hindu polytheism. These women have no contact with men even of their own communities, much less with Western men or missionaries. The best way for the Christian message to reach them is through missionary women.

While in East Pakistan, Jean Baugh found opportunities to witness as she invited teachers from the government school to her home for tea. In one afternoon she entertained women from as many as four different religious backgrounds. She was able to get a Hindu, a Buddhist, and a Muslim around her "Christian pot of tea." She would probably never have been able to get them inside the church.

Jane Moore found that the Pakistani wives like to come to her home each week for Bible study. They have not yet learned to use all of their new freedoms, and by Mrs. Moore's example they learn Bible truths while learning to take responsibilities in proclaiming the Christian message.

Betty Cummins felt that showing what a Christian home is really like was her best method of witnessing to Pakistani women. Shielded behind the purdah veil or screen all their lives, they are cut off from the social world. Also, the Muslim wife may have to share her home with as many as three other wives.

Marjorie Bennett has many opportunities of witnessing. In Dacca she helped in the reading room at a Baptist center which is trying to reach the twenty thousand university students in Dacca. In addition, she taught in the English-speaking Sunday School started by American laymen. She has worked in Comilla the last four years.

Betty Johnson and Betty McKinley also find that the Christian home is their major opportunity to witness. Of course, they are called upon to serve in many ways in the local churches, in schools, and with "mission correspondence." Through genuine friendships, Christ may lead the Pakistani women to himself.

Even though it may be physically straining and frustrating, Dr. Jeanne (Mrs. Charles) Beckett will be able to witness both through her Christian home and in the practice of medicine. Since most Muslim women would never go to a male doctor, Jeanne need not "work to build up a practice." As she ministers to the women's physical needs, she may gain their confidence and earn for herself the privilege of a broader and deeper spiritual ministry.

Missionary women know they may not be able to report in statistics the results of their work. Few Pakistani wives will change their religion unless their husbands do. But the witness of humble Muslim and Hindu wives may incline their husbands or, more likely, their young sons toward accepting the Christian message. In a land where the birth of girl babies is often considered unfortunate, perhaps Pakistani girls may realize their real worth to the kingdom of God as Bible women, Christian nurses or teachers, or even as Christian homemakers.

Missionaries in East Pakistan often find evangelistic outlets by taking preaching tours by boat along the many waterways, by passing out Christian literature at Hindu festivals, and by preaching in the various churches. Whether or not a mission's work is successful depends on a thousand little things. Sometimes the missionary's attitude toward other races and nationalities decides whether or not men come to Christ through his ministry. The clever Pakistani can easily sense whether he is really accepted "as one in Christ," or if the foreigner holds deep-seated racial prejudice and a feeling of superiority. Whatever may be the missionary's verbal testimony, or even actions regarding these matters, his inner attitude shows through.

Open doors to other nations may depend upon how a student or tourist is treated while he is in the United States. Missionary James McKinley can testify to this. He expressed to Dr. Winston Crawley, Southern Baptists' secretary for the Orient, his desire to meet a certain government official in a nearby district that has not one evangelical witness among its 2,500,000 people. A little later, when McKinley and Dr. Crawley went to the railway station, a Pakistani man approached

McKinley and asked him to get a piece of trash out of his eye. This was the man Mr. McKinley had wanted to meet! It was a friendly, informal way to meet an important official. What really made it possible was the fact that while in the States the Pakistani man was treated in a very hospitable and friendly way. Had Americans not been courteous to this one Pakistani, they could have closed the door on more than two million people. The way Americans treat international students may well mean advance or failure of our missionaries.

Nationals seldom expect foreigners to accept their religion. Indians do not expect people from abroad to be Hindus. They accept differences graciously. Muslims do not blame an American for not being a Muslim. As a Christian foreigner, the missionary will be treated courteously and respected as a "holy man." While neither Muslim nor Hindu expects missionaries to accept his religion, each expects, and rightfully, to be accepted as a person. Only on this basis is there an opening for the Christian witness. Only then will all barriers be erased and God's Spirit be able to do his work.

This truth was brought home to me once as I extolled to an Indian colleague the virtues of a very notable missionary. This missionary had done outstanding work, and he gave marvelous messages in the pulpit. When I finished praising him, my friend looked at me and said: "You foreigners do not understand us. I want to tell you something I have never breathed before. That man has labored among us for years. He may be a success in Western terms of success. But he has never accepted even one of us as his equal. He always holds a snobbish distance above us. He has given much, but he gave it condescendingly. He shares with us, but always on his own terms. He is God's representative to many of us. Is God like him?"

Practically in tears because of his earnestness and the pathos in his voice, I was reminded of the thirteenth chapter of I Corinthians—"and have not love." Continuing to listen to his discerning portrait of my deflated hero, I breathed a prayer of thanksgiving to God for this lesson early in my missionary career.

The Christian witness is not just an act or a word. It is the sum total of all that is said and done, of all that the Christian's life reflects. How Christians in America treat Indians and Pakistanis can determine the effectiveness of the Christian mission in the subcontinent in a very strategic way. The missionary himself must stay on his toes spiritually so that not even one offensive act or haughty look will nullify the multitude of good things he does.

The urgency of reinforcing our efforts in East Pakistan is pressing. How long the wide-open door to this large Muslim nation will remain open, no one knows. In no other area of the world do such large numbers of people have so few evangelical witnesses. There is only one evangelical Christian per twenty-five hundred people. Southern Baptists are the only major American denomination working there. What if their efforts are too little and too late? Even if as many as fifty Southern Baptist preachers should go to East Pakistan, they would each have at least a million people to preach to.

Southern Baptists have eight preachers for approximately fifty million people in East Pakistan. Fourteen of the states in the United States each have over one thousand Southern Baptist preachers. Is this due to the injustice of God? No. It is due to the unresponsiveness of his people. Southern Baptists have contact with West Pakistan only when jet planes touch down at the Karachi airport before speeding their missionaries and tourists off to other Asian countries. When a man has an encounter with smallpox, he is forced to bear its marks for the rest of his life. Why is it that when a man has a face-lifting encounter with Christ, he often fails voluntarily to bear witness to its effects on his life?

Christ "looked out upon the multitudes and had compassion." He sent his first disciples unto the "uttermost parts of the earth." Many of his present-day disciples look out and merely aspire to be pastor of First Baptist Church, Somewhere, U.S.A.

# 5 The Look Beyond

Ah, but a man's reach should exceed his grasp,
Or what's a heaven for?

ROBERT BROWNING

For centuries majestic Mount Everest, more than five miles high, has towered over the subcontinent. Queen of a thousand peaks in the Himalayas, she is a land of eternal snows. Her deep ravines and steep, icy slopes have challenged men to risk their lives for the prize of standing atop her uppermost peak. Many have lost their footing and remained along the slopes and crevices in a permanent deep freeze. Yet, men continue to climb as enthusiastically as if God were sitting on top of the mountain and they could literally climb into his presence.

Beneath the Himalayas and the home of the "abominable snowman," beyond the winding trails of Khyber Pass, lies another magnificent piece of God's handiwork. Stretching out over miles and miles of mountains, plains, and lush lowlands, the subcontinent has a quality of durability. The underlying foundation of the entire subcontinent seems to be one huge rock with many "rocklets" of various sizes scattered liberally over her surface.

Huge masses of rock from the land's understructure have stood on the surface for centuries, seemingly permanently separated from the "mother mass." Civilization has worn the surface smooth, but the stones still stand. Men have chiseled everything from temples to life-sized elephants to building blocks out of the surplus rocks, but still the supply is abundant. Some people have jokingly suggested that Jesus was speaking of India when he said, "Upon this rock I will build my church." Artists of every generation have adorned the borders of this stone with their varied expressions, some of them so real that they startle a newcomer.

In central India skinny, hungry cattle try to snatch every twig or blade of green before it is roasted against the ever-near chunks of stone. Along the rivers and coast the rock is covered by several feet of rich soil and luxuriant tropical growth. Here and there, and even out in the sea, boulders of rock sit singly to remind one of its underlying presence.

This rock structure is a symbol of the durability of the subcontinent's people. Whether they be Pakistani or Indian, they give foreigners the impression that whatever may come they will adapt and survive some way or another. It may be the 120-degree heat of the plains or the iciness of the north, the epidemics of smallpox or cholera, the ravages of flood or famine, but they bind their wounds, bury their dead, and act as if procreation were the solution of all these problems. And when it is all over, the people seem more numerous than when the difficulty came. Even when the slaughter took so many at the time of the partitioning of the subcontinent, the population was restored within less than two months. Ten million babies annually join this battle of "survival of the fittest."

In the subcontinent as many people are well educated, cultured, and comfortably housed, fed, and clothed as in the United States, but one is unaware of it. The percentage makes the difference. About 150,000,000 people in India and Pakistan enjoy these comforts and benefits. In fact, some of the world's richest people live in those countries. At the same time 450,000,000 live on as little as four to twenty cents a day. Some eat only one meal a day. Many are always slightly hungry, some terribly so.

The world's sympathy goes out to these hungry people. And it should. But the more wealthy people should not be forgotten. They have the same spiritual needs and often a spiritual hunger that is even deeper than that of others. The church is the only institution capable of rising above merely humanitarian emotions to a vision of the needs of the whole man.

Until we have identified ourselves with a man's human needs, it is doubtful that we have the right to enter the sanctuary of his soul. In other words, a man will not listen to the gospel if he has had nothing to eat for three days. How can a man hear if pain is drowning out the message? But too often when we give him physical relief his response is so flattering to us that we never cease basking in that. It is appropriate that we should be identified with the superficial strivings of men—for freedom from hunger, injury, disease, tyranny—as long as we do not allow these to obscure our vision of his deeper needs.

It is not just a segment of the subcontinent's need that should challenge Christians. It is all of it. Southern Baptists have only twenty-five missionaries there to work among six hundred million people. Twenty-three are located in East Pakistan and two in India. None are in West Pakistan or the other fringe countries.

There are four facets to the challenge the subcontinent places before Southern Baptists. First, there is the challenge of meeting human needs, of responding to the mere physical requirements of the teeming millions. Second, there is the challenge of sharing the spiritual light which God has given us with thousands who seek to know the true and living God. Third, there is the challenge of seeking more effective ways of getting our message of Christ across the many barriers. Finally, the most difficult and most personal challenge of all is to commit ourselves to the task.

The starting place for evangelism in the subcontinent seems to be in meeting some of the human needs there. We cannot get visas to go to India just to engage in direct evangelism. One must be prepared in some technical way to help in industry, medical work, or social welfare in order to gain entrance to the country. In Pakistan, evangelism is permissible if conducted in an inoffensive way. But anyone with experience in witnessing there knows that the spoken word must be backed up with a demonstration of the love of Christ before the average Pakistani is likely to take note. Just as it is impossible to separate faith and works, so is it impossible to separate witness and involvement with human needs.

As has been mentioned, hunger stalks the subcontinent. Most people there have tasted it; few are secure from it. It is a possibility for everyone. All governments of the countries are concerned about it. Most major world powers have done some work toward helping meet the food deficit. These efforts are noble and have helped —temporarily.

It is beginning to dawn upon most of the "have"

nations of the world that merely giving bread to the "have not" nations fails to solve the problem. The gift must be made in some manner that will not lead the receiver to depend permanently upon the giver. There must be maturity in giving. It must not be done just to meet the givers' need of sharing. It should be done to serve the best interest of the receiver. That is the way Christ gave.

To pass out food during a famine is proper. To continue passing it out so that the farmer sells his oxen, stops planting his wheat, and stops irrigating his land is wrong. Initiative, then, has been replaced with an outstretched hand and a loss of self-respect. The giver has become a curse to the receiver.

Give without obligating the receiver. Help the needy help himself. Such programs on an international scale are the United States Point Four Program, the United States Aid to International Development (USAID) Program, and the Canadian aid programs.

Mention has already been made of the work the Clouds and Smiths did in East Pakistan. They were able to teach Pakistani villagers better ways of working and living. Rather than putting underocean cables for electricity from a Canadian source (to use an exaggerated illustration), Canada sent her experts to help India build dams and hydroelectric power plants on Indian soil. That is mature giving. It leaves India self-sufficient and independent.

Rather than set up a program to send American medical-records librarians to meet the needs of India, the USAID sent someone to train Indian librarians. This someone was Margaret Acker Withus, a Texas Baptist. She went to the medical school at Trivandrum (triv-

VANN-drum), Kerala, for a period of three years and trained several classes of librarians. When she returned to the States the training program was self-sustaining. Mrs. Withus could just as easily have gone to Trivandrum and taken care of the records. It would have cost just about the same amount of money. But when she left, the medical-records libraries of India would have been no better off. She would have given just as much of her time and of herself, but the results of the two approaches are different. This is intelligent giving. In fact, her kind of giving was so outstanding that she was recalled to New Delhi to set up training programs for medical-records librarians in several other centers.

In Vijayawada, in the rich agricultural Telugu area, Mr. and Mrs. Earl Bacon have done a noteworthy piece of work with the USAID Program. These Texans from First Baptist Church in Tyler have helped increase the per-acre crop output to four times what it was before. Agricultural workers with the Indian Government were trained to carry on the same type of work after their teachers returned to America. The Bacons could have spent two years passing out bundles of rice from America. As it is, even after they are gone the lands around that town can feed four times as many mouths. This is planned giving.

Dr. and Mrs. H. A. Henderson, Southern Baptists from Knoxville, Tennessee, are helping in the building of an agricultural university in Bangalore, South India. Because of an enlarging social concern growing out of their Christian experience and commitment, the Hendersons began to look for an opportunity to serve in a developing nation. India's massive population and relative shortage of food made it an ideal place to go.

The opportunity came when the USAID program, in collaboration with the government of India, decided to set up in Bangalore an agricultural university which will definitely influence farming patterns throughout the state of Mysore and probably far beyond its borders.

What does this have to do with Christ, or with the church, or with missions? Much. It is noticeable that all of these people had a Christian motive in going to India with the government programs. Had they not known Christ, they might not have had the incentive to undergo hardships for a needy land and people. Could mission programs not seek out workers for similar areas of service and witness?

Most Indian Christians are villagers, or are only one generation away from the village and have relatives who are still there. Most of them earn their livelihood from the land. The more the land produces, the better chance the farmer will have of feeding his family, supporting the church, sending his children to a Christian school, and sharing with others in need. All these affect the churches and the spread of the gospel. How can there be indigenous churches without self-support, or without trained leadership?

Mr. William Wyler of the Disciples of Christ has caught a vision of the "helpful" type of mission work and is putting it into practice in the Mymensingh district of East Pakistan. His work is lifting the economic prison from around Christian communities. The people with whom he works, often illiterate and ignorant, have heard of such projects before, but they cannot comprehend them until they see the "why's" and "how's" worked out before their eyes. Through demonstration of better farming methods and living conditions, through leadership training schools and group meetings, and through illustrated literature, Mr. Wyler and his Pakistani colleagues are trying to show them that cooperation and improvement in a community can become its security against famine, flood, and other ravages. This is practical Christian giving.

Southern Baptists have some of the best agriculturists in the world. If properly channeled, the efforts of a few of them in Pakistan or India could be a tremendous undergirding force for the kingdom of God. It could be the means whereby the churches in the subcontinent could "get on their feet." This would be a much better witnessing position than "flat of their backs"!

Illiteracy is a terrible hindrance to advancement in the subcontinent. It affects every area of national life, including the churches. Although illiteracy is lower in the Christian areas than in others, there is vast room for improvement even there. Only 18 per cent of the population in Pakistan can read and write. India has a literacy rate of 20 percent.

Throughout the history of the church, it has reached its greatest achievements and purest form when men and women have been able to read the written Word of God. Literacy is of utmost importance in building up the kingdom of God.

There is no greater opportunity open to Christians in the subcontinent than in the field of literacy. Practically everyone from nine to ninety has a passion to learn to read. In a land without television and other distractions there is much time to read. Many who have never heard a sermon are now coming to Christ because they have learned in their remote villages to read of him.

In the East it has been the Christian missionary many

times who has taught the masses how to read. For the
most part, it has been left to Communists to provide the
material to be read. This is true in the subcontinent.
Where Christianity has come, literacy is higher. Where
literacy is highest, communism is strongest. This is startling. Christianity did not bring communism. Certainly
not! But it prepared the ground for reading, and the
"great opportunists" beat us Christians at our own game.
They got there with the most literature after we created
the thirst to read.

Each year, communism pours out to the world five
billion dollars worth of below-cost, attractive literature.
Much of it goes to Asia. While Western nations spend
millions sending out such things as cheese (which most
Indians will not eat), the Communists carefully calculate
where money spent will pay the biggest dividends in
commitment.

What does this mean to Southern Baptists? We have
some of the best schools in the world. We certainly can
produce the best Christian literature available anywhere.
Why can we not turn out literacy workers and literature
specialists to saturate the subcontinent with the "how"
and "what" to read? Obviously, we can. The question
is, will we?

Much has already been said about relief of human
pain, suffering, death. Suffering is awful in the subcontinent. It shatters the most callous Western doctor's
little shell of emotional self-protection. Working there
rudely awakens Western medical personnel, who put
so much emphasis on curative medicine and surgery.
That is because they take for granted the battles by
which preventive medicine and public health have
conquered many diseases in America.

In the subcontinent, the real frontier is preventive medicine and public health. We can grind our lives away taking out lungs destroyed by tuberculosis, but the backlog of cases to be done will only get larger unless someone out on the frontier does something to arrest the spread of tuberculosis. We can work night and day through cholera epidemics, trying to replace the rapid fluid losses, but unless someone is teaching villagers better hygiene, we shall have the same thing to do next year.

We have been able to help a few people, to cure a few, to show Christ's love and compassion to a few. *But he loved all men!* This should broaden our horizon. I am amazed that more specialists in preventive medicine and public health are not on the mission field. They could be instrumental in implementing changes in public health even at the national level. Christian doctors with a real concern could be mighty witnesses if they served with the World Health Organization or any one of the other international organizations interested in preventive measures. Certainly doctors and nurses could, by working in the mission hospitals, do much to bring preventive measures to the local scene. This would put vision in Christian giving.

Such work is important to the Christian cause. A missionary worked for thirty years in a village and won seventeen converts, mostly from the outcaste group. There was a little church, but no money for an outreach. Its witness was expressed only in the daily lives of its members. Then, a typhoid epidemic wiped out the entire group. The missionary had just left for retirement. The visible results of a life's work were erased by the typhoid bacillus! All seventeen people had drunk water from a single contaminated well. One hour spent in boarding up this source of death would have meant more to the cause of Christ in that village than a shipload of powdered milk.

Since all disease cannot be prevented, care must be provided for those who suffer. The Government of India sponsors a fairly extensive health service, with hospitals in all major towns. There are not enough doctors for them yet, but the problem seems to be in training doctors rather than in missionaries doing general medical work. Mission hospitals *are* needed in many large rural areas. There is a real need for mission-sponsored specialty hospitals. The majority of government hospitals do not have specialists in most fields. Mission hospitals with specialists in the broad subjects of medicine, pediatrics, obstetrics and gynecology, and general and thoracic surgery could serve as referral centers for government and smaller mission hospitals. In fact, any other type of new missionary medical work would not likely be accepted in India today.

In East Pakistan, the situation is quite different. There are very few hospitals outside the major cities, and even those have an inadequate bed capacity for the population. Whereas India has one doctor for each 15,000 people, East Pakistan has one for 85,000. India has only one nurse for each 43,000 people, but East Pakistan has only one for every 367,000. If India is considered needy in this respect, Pakistan is destitute.

Any new mission hospitals in the subcontinent must be well staffed with people who at least can measure up to medical standards there. Nursing schools are a "must" in all the hospitals. The governments are anxious to increase the number of nurses in their countries.

It is interesting that, in this area where the average percentage of Christians is 2.3, 80 percent of the nurses are Christians. This is because most Hindu families feel that taking care of another person in any way is the work of the servant class; therefore, only the servant-caste Hindus should do that work. The trouble is that most people of this caste do not have the educational background for nursing. Muslim women, of course, usually are not allowed from behind the veil, much less into the public professions. Most Muslim nurses are men. Only women of the Christian community have broken through these cultural bonds into one of the noblest professions that women can enter. This has given Christian nurses an unusual opportunity to witness that the love of Christ "constraineth us" to enter the medical ministry.

Poverty, the mother of many of the previously mentioned ravages, is epidemic here. It haunts the farmer, the craftsman, the widow, the community, the churches. It stifles hope and starves initiative. It is seen when a dirty, ragged widow tries to thrust her scrawny infant into your arms because she cannot feed or provide for it. It is seen when school children remain away from classes because they lack money for food or clothes or tuition. It is seen when a villager's sole possessions are an earthen vessel for his food, a rough homewoven cloth to cover his nakedness, and a scarf to keep the night air from his head. To three hundred million people in the subcontinent success consists of mere survival.

I saw poverty most graphically when a young intern told me his story. He had seen bad crop years before, but this year brought a complete failure. There was no food. His family had gone to bed hungry for six months.

As a last resort, they wrote and asked him to find work to help them. I asked if they could not hold out just for the six months he lacked before finishing his internship. He replied that they had gone as far as they could before appealing to him. They needed only about ten dollars a month to survive. On the verge of his leaving for home, we were able to get a future employer to advance him enough money to feed his family while he finished his training. This is poverty.

Southern Baptists cannot erase poverty from India or Pakistan. The task is too much. But Christ does call us to find ways—lasting ways—of helping to reduce the menace.

Previously, almost all of the poverty I had seen was after the depression of the early 1930's or that associated with alcoholism or laziness or illness. Here, people are caught in circumstances they are powerless to overcome. The Christian governments of the world are about the only agents with purpose, ability, and resources enough to attack the colossal task. As citizens of a Christian government, Southern Baptists could influence and even help plan the strategy for an attack on poverty and hunger. The attack must be centered on remedying the causes rather than on handing out daily loaves.

The second challenge before Southern Baptists is that of sharing the spiritual light of Christ. Some would have us believe that nature itself reveals God. But nature is merely a testimony to his marvelous handiwork. We cannot rely upon nature's testimony to give men the complete picture of God.

Neither can men know God just on the basis of their experiences of life or the conclusions they draw from those experiences. Their conclusions may be drawn upon the wrong premises. Man's interpretations are too self-centered, too much in the "image of man" rather than in the "image of God."

Except for Christianity, all religions are man's attempts at knowing God or understanding himself. They are systems whereby man has tried to interpret nature and experience. We believe that only in Christ has God fully revealed himself to man. Of course, since he created the world and man, his revelation interprets nature and coincides with our experiences as men.

Judaism is a revealed religion, arrested in midstream. Islam and other religions have borrowed revealed elements from Judaism and Christianity. There is truth in them up to a point, but the central Truth, Jesus Christ himself, is conspicuously missing. Christianity has even brought about changes within Hinduism and Hindu society.

The Koran of Islam, which imitates the Bible but eliminates most of its moral teachings, effectually dethrones Christ in the minds of its readers. Mohammed, "the prophet" of Islam, claimed that the Jews and Christians, to whom God's message was given, had lost it and that it was, therefore, given to him. If one looks at the history of Christianity during the seventh century and sees how muddled the message had become in ritual, in priesthood, and in pagan influences, he can better understand Mohammed's reaction to it. What the Christian church of that century had not already muddled, Mohammed masterfully finished muddling as far as the four hundred million Muslims in the world today are concerned.

If God in Christ is revealing himself, Christ has something to say to all men, including those within the

other religions. If Christ has something to say, you and
I must say it. If we must say it, how are we going to
transmit the message? What are our means of communication?

If we are to communicate, we must first realize the
need and the urgency of communicating this message.
The Great Commission of Matthew 28:19-20, Acts 1:8,
and many other passages give us sufficient grounds for
all that we have done or shall ever do to win the
world to Christ. The passage, "There is none other name
under heaven given among men, whereby we must be
saved" (Acts 4:12), should tell us the urgency of communication.

Existing circumstances in the world add their urgency
to our task. Without reviewing all that is involved, it can
be simply stated that communism is on the march
throughout the world and particularly in Asia. Anyone
who knows Marxist doctrine knows that the extinction
of Christianity and of all religions is within the aims of
communism. That should jolt us into action—positive
action for Christ, not just active anticommunism.

Another startling fact is the recent missionary activity
of the world's non-Christian religions. Buddhism is a fad
in some areas of the United States, as well as in the
Orient. Many Buddhist missionaries well grounded in
Christian teachings have been sent to Western countries
in the past few decades. The philosophic variety of
Hinduism has made an unusual appeal to the beatnik
set of intellectuals in the United States. Their seemingly
tolerant, trite expressions of "all roads lead to God" or
"all religions are the same" attract the noncommittal type
of religionist. Both Buddhism and Hinduism make room
for atheism within their philosophies. Islam, always a

missionary faith, is on the march, especially in Africa. Once Islamized, these people are made vastly more resistant to receiving the gospel of Christ.

The insidious effects of secularism in American society and within our churches, and the casual attitude toward great Christian truths among our laity, should arouse us to urgency on the home front. This, in combination with the above facts, should literally shock us into action. The need and the urgency become obvious.

It is the birthright of everyone to know that Christ has offered to redeem him. After that it is his right to accept or reject what has been done for him. God has chosen to trust us with this message of life. He waits on us to proclaim it. Can we say with Paul, "I was not disobedient to the heavenly vision"?

After we accept responsibility to bear witness, the message must be clear and ungarbled. This calls for us to be well grounded in the truths of the Christian faith, especially as they relate to other ideologies. A shallow Christian faith that is concerned only with peace of mind or a church picnic has nothing to say to people who do not have enough to eat.

We must also know well the religion of the people to whom our message is directed. How else can we understand them or put the message in terms they understand? This is not always easy. For instance, there is no word in Tamil for "salvation of sinners."

It has often been said that we must adapt Christ to the Indian or Oriental mind. What utter ignorance! Christ is foreign to no land, alien to no person. What we need to do is to strip our message of its Western cultural trappings. The simple message will speak to the heart of any person, regardless of his race or nation-

ality. The problem is communication. We should let
Asians develop their own forms and expressions of worship. The Eastern Christ will be at home back in the
East. The trouble is, we have often sought to take him
back there in a tuxedo!

Since we come from a wealthy society we often
unconsciously raise material barriers. The person who
worships in a straw *pandal* (PUN-dull, thatch roofed,
open meeting place) does not care to hear about some
Southern Baptist church that has just spent ten thousand
dollars to air-condition the Sunday School annex. Neither
does the village Bible woman, who has never owned a
pair of shoes, get inspiration from hearing a visitor from
America tell of paying sixty dollars for her alligator
shoes and purse. That is more than the Bible woman
receives in a year.

It is proper that we present a message to the individual. This is scriptural. But it brings severe problems to
an Asian who has never made an independent decision.
He is taught from the cradle up to sublimate personal
wishes. The final decision is made by the whole family
or even the entire community. This presents a unique
problem in evangelism. The custom has built a workable
society for Asia, and it has many, many merits. But it
frustrates the Western evangelist who, inexperienced in
the ways of the Orient, expects the aisles to be full by
the end of a week of services. Some would say that we
must break down old cultural walls so that we can do
things here just as we do in the United States. That
attitude creates more walls than it breaks down. Our
attitude should be one that finds ways of penetrating
the walls with the gospel message. The redeeming, re-
generating Christ who touches one individual may

choose also to touch the whole family. Perhaps we should spend more time working toward bringing whole families, or even whole villages, to Christ. The quick baptism of one person from a Hindu family may just as quickly alienate the rest of the family permanently. Since baptism is not necessary for salvation, might it not be delayed while efforts are made through the converted person to reach the rest of the family?

The problem of race, especially, must be faced in mission work. Asia's people identify themselves with the "colored" races of the world. They do not seem to realize that caste and most other prejudices in their own society are based on color or nationality. They are extremely sensitive to any prejudice of a white person toward them. Even some innocent thing may be misinterpreted by them as racial prejudice. We have come preaching that in Christ there is no East or West, that all men are equal before God. They wonder if we practice what we preach.

This last point is a big barrier to the Christian witness the world over. Missionaries, local pastors, church members—all find it difficult, and often fail, to live consistently the faith they speak about. The story is told that some Muslims came to debate with Dr. E. Stanley Jones, a saintly Methodist missionary in India. They were prepared to debate on any ground of theology, theory, or even Bible doctrine. Dr. Jones based his entire appeal on his personal experience with Jesus Christ. The capable Muslim scholars were completely dumbfounded. They knew nothing about a personal experience with Christ or salvation from sin. They could only arise quietly and file out of Dr. Jones's presence because they knew that his life had backed up every word he said.

Men have heard of Jesus. They have seen the symbol
of the cross but still seem puzzled by it. Why? Because
they have seldom seen Christians whose lives show the
self-surrender Christ demonstrated on the cross. Until
they witness him alive in us, Christ will be a mystery
to them. To the Hindu, he will remain only one of many
*avatars* (av-a-TARS, saviors). To the Muslim, he will be
only a lesser prophet, a good teacher, a saintly man.

Many scholars in comparative religions state that the
stone of stumbling in Christianity for Hindus is the
incarnation of Christ as the Son of God. Because they
themselves believe in many incarnations of their gods,
they see Christ as merely one of those. It is said that
for the Muslim the stone of stumbling in Christianity
is the sonship of Christ and the fatherhood of God, because the Muslim mind interprets this as meaning physical relationship.

These are, however, intellectual, philosophical barriers to faith. They correspond to intellectual barriers
the Westerner throws up against belief. At the point of
giving excuses for unbelief, East and West are one. The
real cause of unbelief is universal: the cross of Christ,
which requires total commitment and surrender. The
reason is an unwillingness to let go of moral habits,
cultural patterns, and personal ambition.

Most people, when they think of communications or
channels of missionary witness, think in terms of schools
and hospitals and clinics and a dozen other things.
But the world has never known a channel as powerful
as a life lived in Christ. All other channels we have are
only means of expressing life in Christ more fully.

The best channels, then, are men and women who
have had a profound personal experience with Christ

and have spiritually matured to the point where their lives reflect regeneration and reconciliation. This being so, they will know the elements of their Christian faith. Having a high regard for the importance of the Asians, they will learn Asian philosophy in order to understand them and witness to them. They will give more than lip service to the knowledge that all men are equal before God. They will preach the Word and allow the Holy Spirit to mold lives, rather than expecting lives to be shaped to their stereotyped molds. That means loving people enough to leave them free to accept or reject the message. It means trusting the Holy Spirit to accomplish his work in each life.

One of the marvelous things about Jesus was his teaching methods. Above all, his life was an example of everything he said. The difference between him and the other teachers of his day was that he identified himself with the needs of the men, women, boys, and girls with whom he came in contact. He walked hand in hand with those he taught. He walked, ate, fished, and worshiped with them. As they learned from him, he insisted that they put the teachings into action. This was Christ's way of sharing spiritual light.

He fed, comforted, and healed, but never made food, comfort, and health an end in themselves. His actions were all a part of spiritual enlightenment. He wept, suffered, and died in order to get his message across and to fulfil his mission. By means of his resurrection, he put a permanent source of power behind the light he brought. For Christ's resurrection is the inexhaustible dynamo of power that feeds the incandescent beam of God's eternal revelation of himself and of his love. In order to be true to this light, we must share it.

The third challenge before Southern Baptists is that of finding effective means of witness concerning Christ. The most powerful and effective institution, and the most important means of witness, is the local church; and the primary aim of all undertakings on the mission field is the establishment and undergirding of local churches. These churches must be autonomous in the sense that they would continue to function and witness if all missionaries were withdrawn. They must be centers of evangelism and worship. They should not recede out of contact with society and world issues, but intelligently face and interpret the important questions confronting society. They should provide solutions or at least guidance in finding the answers to all of these issues. Only as the local churches do this will they remain relevant to society and to life. They determine their own usefulness.

If the churches are to be such centers, they must be involved in the life of the communities where they are. Their service must depend on the peculiar need of each area. In one it may be taking care of refugees, in another feeding victims of famine, in another preventing an epidemic, in another education of children who have no school. The churches' opportunities have always exceeded their vision.

Churches of this quality need trained leadership. This calls for Christian schools where leaders may obtain an education in a Christian environment. Religious and theological education must be available and adaptable to the society.

There has never been a time when students were more numerous than they are now in Asia. Churches and missions have unlimited opportunities to provide hostels for

Christian students at non-Christian institutions. Nurtured in Christian growth, those students could be preserved for useful service to God's kingdom. In most Christian schools, and most government schools that have a good number of Christian students, there is real need for student centers with full-time workers. The local churches could do much for students by giving them opportunities of leadership and by providing special holiday retreats for deepening the spiritual life.

A field that has great potential but which has been used very little is that of religious drama. Oriental people like to act and to put on dramatic productions. They are amazingly effective and talented.

Miss Joyce Peel, a British missionary who is a specialist in religious drama, likes to live in the villages with the people. She goes to an area, uses nationals as actors, writes her own scripts as she goes, and captures the Bible messages on stage. After a few nights in one village, she goes on to the next and continues the progressive drama of the biblical message. People follow her from village to village, enthralled with the excitement of the messages and the fact that they are acting. The climax comes as all of the villages pool their talents in a great performance depicting the passion, crucifixion, and resurrection of Christ.

The villagers receive the message. They are so actively involved in the revelation that they never forget the graphic portrayals. Christ to them has become alive. No longer is he just an impersonal god like their stone images in the temples. Hundreds of people who would never have entered a church have received the message in outdoor makeshift sanctuaries. Here lies great potential for the Christian witness.

Villages of the subcontinent, as well as large cities, are adaptable to the small cell-group type of witness. A group could meet with four to eight people studying the Bible together. Then the group could dissolve and each member become the nucleus for another small cell of four to eight. This type of witness would require no equipment or financial backing. It would require only commitment and devotion. The cell leaders could occasionally get together for sharing experiences and for spiritual renewal.

Very little witnessing has been done through mass media. At present there is no television in the subcontinent. Radios are not as common as in Japan, but more and more people are getting them. Often, if there is one radio in a village, all the people gather around it for certain programs. The fact that radio stations are all government-controlled presents certain problems to church groups. But many Christian programs can be picked up from Radio Ceylon, the Far Eastern Broadcasting Company in the Philippines, or from Addis Ababa in Ethiopia. The Far Eastern Broadcasting Company and Gospel Recordings both have studios in Bangalore to produce programs in the Indian languages for use on stations on the outer edge of the subcontinent. The Strict Baptists of England and American Baptists have recording studios.

Almost any program using visual aids or movies will attract a huge audience, whether in village or city. There is a wide-open field for the use of color slides as an adjunct to preaching, or in putting the message across on film alone. It is amazing how much more tolerant people are toward this than they are to direct preaching.

Much already has been said about the need for

Christian literature on a massive scale. Bible correspondence courses are very popular, and not with Christians only. The majority of people who take them are non-Christian seekers who are interested in Christianity but would not at this stage of their quest be seen at a church gathering.

Examples have already been given of the effective work done by Christian laymen in government service. The same can apply to military personnel or tourists, who may do untold good even though their stay be short.

The mission task with the greatest potential is with international students in the United States. Shortly after arriving in India, I received a letter from an Indian man who had recently returned from America with a doctor of philosophy degree from Louisiana State University. He was so impressed by the hospitality and work of the Baptist Student Center at LSU that he offered to do anything possible to help Southern Baptists in India. This type of good will cannot be bought with dollars and cents.

This is only one example among many that Southern Baptist missionaries have experienced. Most international students in the United States return to their own countries to assume very important positions. Their help can influence tremendously the spread of the gospel in their homelands. When any Christian family befriends an international student, they extend their witness across the seas. This could be God's call to you to be a "foreign missionary" right at your own family hearth.

The fourth challenge is personal commitment to the task of winning the subcontinent. Southern Baptists, the largest non-Catholic denomination in America, have the people, the resources, the equipment, the "know-how," and *Christ's command*. All they need in addition is commitment to the task. The subcontinent is there. Many doors are open; Christ holds the keys to others. In a marvelous way he has prepared Southern Baptists for the task. No other group on earth is so well prepared to join with Baptists of India and Pakistan to change the subcontinent in the next generation. It is no longer a question of whether they can. It is whether they will.

A certain range of mountains in India is almost always shrouded by a deep mist rising from the plains. One morning I arose and looked out, and behold! the mist was gone! The snowcapped mountains, fifty miles away, seemed almost within reach. An early morning rain had temporarily dissolved the mist. I had been told of the mountains; now I saw them with my own vision. Even as I gazed upon the gorgeous sight, mist began to enfold the mountains, but I could never forget their reality just beyond the mist.

That is much the way the subcontinent of India and Pakistan seems to many Southern Baptists. It is engulfed in a mist. They know little about it because only recently have they sent missionaries there. But now God has raised the mist for you and you know that the mountainous challenge of India and Pakistan is within reach. That which was behind the mist has been unveiled, and that which was blurred has become reality to you. Do not let this reality slip behind the mist again until you have matched the challenge with your prayers, with your lives, with the lives of your sons and daughters, and with sacrificial gifts from your financial resources.

This is the appointed day for action.

## The Author

Dr. McPhail is a Southern Baptist missionary representative to India. His native state is Mississippi.

At the time of his missionary appointment in October of 1961, Dr. McPhail was surgeon at Scott County Hospital in Morton, Mississippi. Before that, he was first an intern and then a surgery resident at University Hospital, Jackson, Mississippi. In the summer of 1955 he was a student missionary in Juarez, Mexico, for the Texas Baptist Student Union.

Dr. McPhail attended Clarke Memorial College in Newton, Mississippi, and received a bachelor of science degree from Mississippi College in Clinton. He received the doctor of medicine degree from Baylor University College of Medicine, Houston, Texas, and also attended Southwestern Baptist Theological Seminary in Fort Worth.

Originally appointed for Nigeria, Dr. and Mrs. McPhail were reassigned when an opportunity came to enter India. They are the first missionaries of the Southern Baptist Foreign Mission Board to serve in India.

THE EDITOR

## Pronunciations

(Others are included in text)

Aryan—AIR-eh-ann
Bangalore—BANG-gah-lohr
Bhutan—buh-TAHN
Cochin—CO-chin
Comilla—coo-MEEL-ah
Dacca—DOCK-ah
Delhi—DELL-ey
Dravidian—dra-VID-ey-an
Faridpur—fah-REED-poor
Feni—FEH-nee
Hooghly—HOO-gley
Jummu—JUM-oo
Kerala—CUR-uh-luh
Khyber—KIGH-burr
Madras—mah-DRAHS
Malayalam—mal-ah-YAH-lam
Mymensingh—MY-men-sing
Nepal—neh-PAUL
Noakhali—no-occ-HAH-ly
Pabna—PUB-nah
Pakistan—pack-ey-STAN or pah-ky-STAHN
Parsee—PAHR-see
Punjab—pun-JOB
Rajbari—rahj-BAH-ry
Serampore—SEH-rahm-pour
Sikkim—SICK-im
Sirajganj—sir-RAHJ-gunj
Telugu—TELL-uh-goo
Tripura—TRIP-oo-rah
Vellore—veh-LOHR

## Questions

*Chapter 1*

1. Describe some of the racial and cultural differences among people in the subcontinent.
2. Who were the Dravidians? the Aryans?
3. What is meant by the "caste system"?
4. Characterize the rule of Asoka.
5. Why was the country of Pakistan created?

*Chapter 2*

6. What is a Hindu "joint family"? What are its advantages? its disadvantages?
7. What is the name of the sacred writings of Hinduism? of Islam?
8. How does Dr. McPhail answer these charges Indians make?

     (1) "All roads lead to God"?
     (2) "Christians are too exclusive"?
     (3) "Christianity is dogmatic"?

9. Is it true that Westerners are material-minded and Easterners spiritual-minded?
10. Why has communism made its greatest appeal among intellectuals in the subcontinent?

*Chapter 3*

11. Who is said to have been the first missionary to India?
12. Who were the first Protestant missionaries to the subcontinent? When did they go there?
13. Who was the first Baptist missionary? When did he go out?

14. Who were the first Baptist missionaries from the United States?

15. Name some other Baptist groups that have missionaries in the subcontinent.

## Chapter 4

16. Outline the differences between East and West Pakistan.

17. When did the first Southern Baptist missionaries enter Pakistan? Who were they?

18. What connection did Southern Baptist work have with that of Australian Baptists?

19. Name four Pakistani cities where Southern Baptist missionaries are located and characterize the type of work in each.

20. Why are missionary women of special importance to the spread of the gospel in a Muslim country?

## Chapter 5

21. How many missionaries do Southern Baptists have in the subcontinent?

22. What are the four facets of the challenge the subcontinent places before Southern Baptists?

23. Why must missionaries to India have special preparation in some secular work? Is the same requirement made of missionaries to Pakistan?

24. What is the primary channel of missionary witness?

25. What is the primary aim of all undertakings on the mission field?